AWS

The Ultimate Step-by-Step Guide from beginners to Advanced for Amazon Web Services

Disclaimer Notice:

including, but not limited to, — errors, omissions, or inaccuracies.

Table of Contents

CHAPTER 1

What Is AWS?

Distributed Computing With AWS

Amazon Web Services (AWS) is the world's generally extensive and comprehensively received cloud stage, offering more than 175 completely highlighted administrations from server farms all-inclusive. A huge number of clients—including the quickest developing new companies, biggest undertakings, and driving government organizations—are utilizing AWS to bring down costs, become progressively lithe, and enhance quicker.

Most Usefulness

AWS has altogether more administrations, and more highlights inside those administrations, than some other cloud supplier from framework advances like figure, stockpiling, and databases–to developing advances, for example, AI and computerized reasoning, information lakes and investigation, and Internet of Things. This makes it quicker, simpler, and savvier to move your current applications to the cloud and construct about anything you can envision.

AWS additionally includes the most profound usefulness inside those administrations. For instance, AWS offers the vastest assortment of databases that are reason worked for various sorts of utilizations so you can pick the correct instrument for the activity to get the best cost and execution.

The biggest people group of clients and accomplices

AWS has the biggest and most powerful network, with a huge number of dynamic clients and a huge number of accomplices internationally. Clients crosswise over essentially every industry and of each size, including new companies, ventures, and open part associations, are running each comprehensible use case on AWS. The AWS Partner Network (APN) incorporates a large number of frameworks integrators who have practical experience in AWS administrations and a huge number of free programming sellers (ISVs) who adjust their innovation to chip away at AWS.

Generally Secure

AWS is architected to be the most adaptable and secure distributed computing condition accessible today. Our center framework is worked to fulfill the security necessities for the military, worldwide banks, and other high-affectability associations. This is supported by a profound arrangement of cloud security instruments, with 230 security, consistency, and administration administrations and highlights. AWS bolsters 90 security gauges and consistence accreditations, and every one of the 117 AWS administrations that store client information offers the capacity to scramble that information.

Quickest Pace of Advancement

With AWS, you can use the most recent advancements to analyze and improve all the more rapidly. We are ceaselessly quickening our pace of advancement to create altogether new innovations you can use to change your business. For instance, in 2014, AWS spearheaded the serverless processing space with the dispatch of AWS Lambda, which lets designers run their code without provisioning or overseeing servers. Furthermore, AWS constructed Amazon SageMaker, a completely overseen AI administration that engages regular designers and researchers to utilize AI with no past experience.

Most Demonstrated Operational Skill

AWS has the unrivaled experience, development, unwavering quality, security, and execution that you can rely on for your most significant applications. For more than 13 years, AWS has been conveying cloud administrations to a great many clients around the globe running a wide assortment of utilization cases. AWS has the most operational experience, at a more prominent scale, of any cloud supplier.

Worldwide System of AWS Regions

AWS has the broadest worldwide cloud foundation. No other cloud supplier offers the same number of Regions with various Availability Zones associated with low inactivity, high throughput, and exceptionally excess systems administration. AWS has 69

Availability Zones inside 22 geographic areas around the globe and has declared designs for 13 greater Availability Zones and four more AWS Regions in Indonesia, Italy, South Africa, and Spain. The AWS Region/Availability Zone model has been perceived by Gartner as the suggested methodology for running venture applications that require high accessibility.

CHAPTER 2

History Of AWS

A Brief History of AWS

Now and again, it can feel like the ~$120 billion cloud industry rose out of nowhere, apparently medium-term. Yet, Amazon Web Services (AWS), the spearheading (and driving) distributed computing stage gave by Amazon.com, rose up out of independent interior activities at Amazon more than 15 years back to both guide designers and furthermore improve the productivity of the organization's very own foundation.

The sources of AWS as a designer device can be followed right back to 2002, when an underlying beta was discharged (named Amazon.com Web Service) that offered SOAP and XML interfaces for the Amazon item index. This doormat for designers was the initial step by Amazon to grasping the capability of engineer agreeable instruments, especially in a foundation space, as a real item.

Not long after, in 2003, during an official retreat at Jeff Bezos' home, the Amazon administration group was solicited to distinguish the center qualities from the organization. One thing turned out to be inexhaustibly clear: Its frameworks administrations gave them an immense preferred position over their opposition.

From that point, a more fabulous thought rose: That a blend of framework administrations and designer apparatuses could turn into a pseudo-working framework for the web. By detaching various pieces of the framework (register power, stockpiling, and database) as parts to the working framework and having engineer well-disposed instruments to oversee them, it was conceivable to think about the foundation (particularly Amazon's) as computerized and institutionalized with web benefits that can call for more assets. In 2004, the organization's first open affirmation of AWS rose in a blog entry, alluding to the advancements to come.

Openly propelled on March 19, 2006, AWS offered Simple Storage Service (S3) and Elastic Compute Cloud (EC2), with Simple Queue Service (SQS) following before long. By 2009, S3 and EC2 were propelled in Europe, the Elastic Block Store (EBS) was made open, and an incredible substance conveyance organizes (CDN), Amazon CloudFront, all became proper pieces of AWS advertising. These designer benevolent administrations pulled in cloud-prepared clients and put everything out on the table for formalized associations with information-hungry ventures, for example, Dropbox, Netflix, and Reddit, all before 2010.

There are bunches of tales about the development of AWS, however, this much we know: 10 years back, Amazon Web Services, the cloud Infrastructure as a Service arm of Amazon.com, was propelled with little ballyhoo as a side business for Amazon.com. Today, it's a profoundly fruitful organization in its own right, riding a noteworthy $10 billion run rate.

Truth be told, as indicated by information from Synergy Research, in the decade since its dispatch, AWS has developed into the best cloud foundation organization on earth, collecting in excess of 30 percent of the market. That is more than its three nearest equals — Microsoft, IBM, and Google — joined (and by a reasonable edge).

An outline from Synergy Research with Infrastructure as a Service piece of the pie.

What you cannot deny is that the roots for the possibility of AWS return to the 2000 time period when Amazon was a far unexpected organization in comparison to it is today — just an internet business organization battling with scale issues. Those issues constrained the organization to assemble some strong inner frameworks to manage the hyper development it was encountering — and that established the framework for what might become AWS.

Talking as of late at an occasion in Washington, DC, AWS CEO Andy Jassy, who has been there from the earliest starting point, clarified how these center frameworks created out of need over a three-year time span starting in 2000, and, before they knew it, with no genuine arranging, they had the makings of a business that would become AWS.

Making Inward Frameworks

It started path, thinking back to the 2000 time allotment when the organization needed to dispatch a web-based business administration called Merchant.com to help outsider vendors like Target or Marks and Spencer assemble web-based shopping destinations over Amazon's online business motor. It ended up being much harder than they suspected to construct an outside advancement stage, since, in the same way as other new companies, when it propelled in 1994, it didn't generally design well for future prerequisites. Rather than a composed improvement condition, they had unwittingly made a disordered chaos. That made it an immense test to isolate the different administrations to make a brought together improvement stage that would be valuable for outsiders.

So discreetly around 2000, we turned into an administration organization with actually no exhibit.

By then, the organization ventured out building the AWS business by unwinding that chaos into a lot of well-archived APIs. While it drove the smoother improvement of Merchant.com, it likewise served the inside designer group of spectators well, as well, and it set up for a significantly more sorted out and taught a method for creating devices inside going ahead.

"We expected every one of the groups inside starting thereon to work in a decoupled, API-get to design, and afterward the entirety of the inward groups within Amazon expected to have the option to expend their companion interior improvement group benefits in that manner. So unobtrusively around 2000, we turned into an administration organization with actually no ballyhoo," Jassy said.

At about a similar time, the organization was developing rapidly and procuring new programming architects, yet they were all the while finding, disregarding the extra individuals, they weren't building applications any quicker. When Jassy, who was Amazon CEO Jeff Bezos' head of staff at the time, dove into the issue, he found a running grievance. The official group anticipated that a task should take three months; however, it was taking three months just to construct the database, process or capacity part. Everybody was building their very own assets for an individual undertaking, with no idea to scale or reuse. (I figure you can think about where this is going.)

The interior groups at Amazon required a lot of basic foundation administrations everybody could access without rehashing an already solved problem unfailingly, and that is absolutely what Amazon set out to manufacture — and that is the point at which they started to acknowledge they may have something greater.

Jassy recounts an official retreat at Jeff Bezos' home in 2003. It was there that the official group led an activity distinguishing the organization's center skills — an activity they expected to most recent 30 minutes, yet wound up going on a reasonable piece longer. Obviously, they realized they had aptitudes to offer a wide choice of items, and they were great at satisfying and sending orders, yet when they began to burrow they understood they had these different abilities they hadn't considered.

All things considered, it appears to be genuinely self-evident; however, at the time I don't think we had ever truly disguised that.

As the group worked, Jassy reviewed, they understood they had likewise gotten very great at running framework administrations like process, stockpiling and database (due to those recently verbalized interior necessities).

Additionally, they had gotten exceptionally talented at running solid, adaptable, financially savvy server farms out of need. As a low-edge professional Amazon, they must be as lean and productive as could be expected under the circumstances.

It was by then, without even completely articulating it that they began to figure what AWS could be, and they started to think about whether they had an extra business giving framework administration to engineers.

"By and large it appears to be genuinely self-evident, however, at the time, I don't think we had ever truly disguised that," Jassy clarified.

The Working Framework for the Web

They didn't actually have an "Aha" minute, however, they began to expand on the underlying chunk of a thought that started at the retreat — and in the Summer of 2003, they began to think about this arrangement of administrations as a working arrangement of sorts for the web. Keep in mind; this is as yet three years before they propelled AWS, so it was a thought that would set aside an effort to prepare.

"On the off chance that you accept organizations will assemble applications without any preparation over the foundation administrations if the correct choice [of services] existed, and we accepted they would in the event that the correct choice existed, at that point the working framework turns into the web, which is extremely unique in relation to what had been the situation for the [previous] 30 years," Jassy said.

That prompted another talk about the parts of this working framework, and how Amazon could help construct them. As they investigated further, by the Fall of 2003 they reasoned this was a Greenfield where every one of the segments required to run the web OS presently couldn't seem to be constructed — so, all in all, I'm envisioning their eyes lit up.

"We understood we could contribute those key parts of that web working framework, and with that, we went to seek after this a lot more extensive strategic, is AWS today, which is true to permit any association or organization or any designer to run their innovation applications over our innovation foundation stage."

At that point they set out to do only that — and the rest, as it's been said, is history. A couple of years after the fact the organization propelled their Infrastructure as a Service (a term that most likely didn't exist until some other time). It required some investment for the plan to grab hold; however, today it's a profoundly rewarding business.

AWS was first to advertise with an advanced cloud framework administration when it propelled Amazon Elastic Compute Cloud in August 2006. Shockingly, it took quite a while before a contender reacted. In that capacity, they control a tremendous measure of a piece of the pie, in any event until further notice. Have confidence, some very well-obeyed contenders like Microsoft, Google, IBM and others are gunning for them.

When inquired as to whether he at any point anticipated the achievement they've accomplished, Jassy was modest, saying, "I don't consider any us had the boldness to foresee it would develop as large or as quick as it has."

In any case, given how the organization painstakingly laid the foundation for what might become AWS, you need to imagine that they saw something here that no one else did, a thought that they accepted could be gigantic. As it turned out, what they saw was nothing, not exactly the fate of registering.

CHAPTER 3

Getting Started With AWS

Prepared to find out additional? Associate with the AWS engineer network, advance your insight with on the web and in-person training, exhibit your ability with confirmations, and investigate reference materials to assist you with expanding on AWS.

Interface With Engineer Networks

The worldwide AWS environment comprises of a scope of AWS aficionados and backers who are enthusiastic about helping other people construct.

Client Gatherings

Join an AWS people group close to you to learn, system, and offer your enthusiasm for distributed computing.

AWS Heroes

Find out about the lively overall network of master clients and influencers.

Virtual People Group

Add your voice to the AWS dialogs occurring in different online networks.

AWS Events

Interface, work together and gain from specialists at on the web and in-person AWS occasions.

Develop Your Range of Abilities

Regardless of whether you are only inquisitive about AWS or a prepared star, you have a huge information base available to you.

AWS Online Tech Talks

Stream online introductions and workshops drove by AWS arrangements modelers and specialists.

AWS Partner Network TV

Watch sessions, meetings, demos, and all the more including AWS and APN Partners.

Get Prepared and Confirmed

Gain from AWS specialists. Advance your aptitudes and information. Manufacture your future in the AWS Cloud.

Computerized and Study Hall Preparing

Learn with free computerized preparing or increase hands-on involvement with a live homeroom.

Accreditation Tests

Acquire qualifications and exhibit your AWS aptitude to bosses and companions.

Investigate Reference Materials

Convenient reference materials to assist you with expanding on AWS.

CHAPTER 4

What Is Cloud Computing?

Basically, distributed computing is the conveyance of processing administrations—including servers, stockpiling, databases, organizing, programming, investigation, and insight—over the Internet ("The Cloud") to offer quicker development, adaptable assets, and economies of scale. You normally pay just for cloud administrations you use, helping bring down your working costs, run your foundation all the more proficiently and scale as your business needs change.

Top Advantages of Distributed Computing

Distributed computing is a major move from the conventional way organizations consider IT assets. Here are seven normal reasons associations are going to distributed computing administrations:

Cost

Distributed computing takes out the capital cost of purchasing equipment and programming and setting ready for action nearby datacenters—the racks of servers, the nonstop power for power and cooling, the IT specialists for dealing with the foundation. It includes quick.

Speed

Most distributed computing administrations are given self-help and on request, so even immense measures of figuring assets can be provisioned in minutes, ordinarily with only a couple of mouse clicks, giving organizations a ton of adaptability and easing the heat off scope quantification.

Worldwide Scale

The advantages of distributed computing administrations incorporate the capacity to scale flexibly. In cloud talk, that implies conveying the perfect measure of IT assets—for instance, pretty much processing force, stockpiling, transfer speed—right when it is required and from the privilege geographic area.

Profitability

On location datacenters regularly require a great deal of "Racking and stacking"—equipment arrangement, programming fixing, and other tedious IT the board tasks. Distributed computing evacuates the requirement for a large number of these undertakings, so IT groups can invest energy in accomplishing increasingly significant business objectives.

Execution

The greatest distributed computing administrations run on an overall system of secure datacenters, which are normally moved up to the most recent age of quick and effective registering equipment. This offers a few advantages over a solitary corporate datacenter, including diminished system idleness for applications and more prominent economies of scale.

Unwavering Quality

Distributed computing makes information reinforcement, catastrophe recuperation and business progression simpler and more affordable in light of the fact that information can be reflected at various excess destinations on the cloud supplier's system.

Security

Many cloud suppliers offer an expansive arrangement of strategies, advancements, and controls that reinforce your security pose, by and large, ensuring your information, applications and foundation from potential dangers.

Kinds of Distributed Computing

Not all mists are the equivalent and not one kind of distributed computing is directly for everybody. A few distinct models, types and administrations have developed to help offer the correct answer for your needs.

Initially, you have to decide the sort of cloud arrangement or distributed computing design that your cloud administrations will be actualized on. There are three distinct approaches to send cloud administrations: on an open cloud, private cloud or half and half cloud.

Open Cloud

Open mists are claimed and worked by an outsider cloud specialist organizations, which convey their processing assets like servers and capacity over the Internet. Microsoft Azure is a case of an open cloud. With an open cloud, all equipment, programming, and other supporting foundation are possessed and overseen by the cloud supplier. You get to these administrations and deal with your record utilizing an internet browser.

Private Cloud

A private cloud alludes to distributed computing assets utilized only by a solitary business or association. A private cloud can be physically situated on the organizations on location datacenter. A few organizations likewise pay outsider specialist co-ops to have their private cloud. A private cloud is one in which the administrations and framework are kept up on a private system.

Half and Half Cloud

Half and half mists join open and private mists, bound together by innovation that enables information and applications to be shared between them. By enabling information and applications to move among private and open mists, a half breed cloud gives your business more prominent adaptability, greater arrangement choices and enhances your current foundation, security, and consistency.

CHAPTER 5

Advantages Of AWS

Regularly individuals ask for convincing reasons for what reason they ought to consider AWS for their foundation needs. In spite of the fact that there are hundreds and thousands of clients influence AWS in excess of 190 nations, with several contextual analyses including organizations like Netflix, Pinterest, Dow Jones, SAP, Coursera, NASA/JPL, Reddit, Vodafone, 99Designs, Thomson Reuters, Flipboard, Expedia and LinkedIn yet the greater part of the individuals who are dealing with their foundation in-house or a co-found server farm, may at present have worries around cost, security, information protection and some more.

In this blog, I have recorded what I see as the top 10 advantages of utilizing AWS for your foundation needs:

1. Zero CapEx:

Numerous individuals will, in general, accept that AWS or some other cloud-based arrangement is just for the wealthy. Be that as it may, the fact of the matter is direct inverse. We see AWS as playing field leveler empowering new companies to use very good quality innovations and foundation needs with ZERO CapEx. New businesses avoiding utilizing Oracle as their database or some other plugs virtual products that request high-forthright authorizing cost must investigate AWS Marketplace and in high-likelihood, they may discover those items in an hourly estimated model with no straightforward expense.

2. No-Commitment:

Regardless of whether you require a server for facilitating a little site, a Content Delivery Network (CDN) for substantial traffic destinations, solid and adaptable email administration, information warehousing administration, or Hadoop group for your BigData needs, AWS offers everything with definitely no-dedication by any stretch of the imagination, not by any means a month. All server-supported administrations are charged on an hourly premise, so when you end/stop a server, you won't be charged from one hour from now.

3. Dispose of Negotiations:

Definitely value exchanges aren't an ability region for some (at least me) and neither one of us likes investing our time and vitality doing that regardless of whether we have what it takes. AWS is profoundly centered around lessening foundation costs for their clients.

They have discounted they're evaluating crosswise over different administrations in excess of multiple times in the most recent couple of years. Apparatuses like Trusted Advisor, or outsider instruments like CloudCheckr, Cloudability, Cloudyn and so forth can give you bits of knowledge to enhance cost inside your current arrangement on AWS.

4. Acquisition:

Acquiring another server may require some investment between a few hours to 8-10 days relying on whether your foundation is on-premise, co-found or in the event that you are related with a facilitating supplier. Comparable time is expected to get programming licenses also. Nonetheless, AWS empowers you to turn up new servers inside a couple of moments with no compelling reason to purchase separate licenses for some working frameworks and programming projects.

5. Pay Per Use:

Consider unbounded space for your reinforcement and authentic needs, the capacity to dispatch new servers, up-scale/downscale a server, CDN combination, transcoding media records, boundless data transfer capacity and a lot more profoundly adaptable administrations/highlights accessible to you while you pay depends on your real use as it were.

6. Security:

AWS has fabricated a world-class, exceptionally secure framework, both physically and over the web. Scarcely any features from the safety efforts referenced on AWS site are:

Server farms are staffed 24×7 via prepared security monitors, and access is approved carefully on a least special premise

Various geographic locales and Availability Zones enable you to stay versatile even with most disappointment modes, including catastrophic events or framework disappointments

Capacity to arrange worked in firewall rules from absolutely open to totally private or someplace in the middle of to control access to occasions.

Influence Identity and Access Management (IAM) and CloudTrail to hold the track to all exercises done by various clients.

Hardly any different features incorporate private subnets, Multi-factor confirmation (MFA), Isolate GovCloud and scrambled information stockpiling.

7. Adaptability:

Disregard mystery or logical examination to distinguish your foundation needs. You can use auto-scaling to construct a self-overseeing foundation adjusted near the genuine need dependent on traffic/asset usage. Amazon Machine Images (AMIs) empowers you to turn up clones in various districts for various conditions inside a couple of moments, wiping out the need to rehash the set-up steps unfailingly.

8. Worldwide Leader:

Amazon has worldwide nearness with 10 districts, 36 accessibility zones and in excess of 50 edge areas. Scarcely any months back, Gartner situated AWS in Leaders Quadrant of the new Magic Quadrant for Cloud Infrastructure as a Service. Gartner likewise referenced that AWS has in excess of multiple times the figure limit being used than the total aggregate of rest 14 specialist organizations set in a similar Magic Quadrant.

9. Top tier PaaS Offerings:

AWS has thought of exceptionally adaptable oversaw administrations for database, reserving, information warehousing, transcoding, capacity, reinforcement, foundation the board and application the executives, which diminish the general time and exertion spent in setting-up and dealing with the framework and in this manner significantly diminishing the go-to-showcase cycle for end-clients.

10. Programming interface:

APIs are accessible in different programming dialects to assist you in dealing with your framework automatically. Regardless of whether it implies propelling another case, or taking reinforcements, the sky is the limit through API. Truth be told, APIs are more dominant than the AWS Management Console.

Six Advantages of Cloud Computing

Exchange capital cost for variable cost – Instead of putting vigorously in server farms and servers before you realize how you're going to utilize them, you can pay just when you devour registering assets, and pay just for the amount you expend.

Advantage from gigantic economies of scale – By utilizing distributed computing, you can accomplish a lower variable expense than you can jump individually. Since utilization from a huge number of clients is collected in the cloud, suppliers, for example, AWS can accomplish higher economies of scale, which converts into lower follow through on as-you-go costs.

Quit speculating limit – Eliminate speculating on your framework limit needs. At the point when you settle on a limit choice preceding sending an application, you frequently end up either sitting on costly inactive assets or managing constrained limits. With distributed computing, these issues leave. You can access to such an extent or as meager limit as you need, and scale here and there as required with just a couple of moments' notification.

Speed up and nimbleness – In a distributed computing condition, new IT assets are just a tick away, which implies that you lessen an opportunity to make those assets accessible to your designers from weeks to only minutes. These outcomes in an emotional increment in dexterity for the association, since the expense and time it takes to test and create, is fundamentally lower.

Quit going through cash running and keeping up server farms – Focus on ventures that separate your business, not the framework. Distributed computing lets you center around your very own clients, instead of on the hard work of racking, stacking, and controlling servers.

Go worldwide in minutes – Easily convey your application in numerous districts the world over with only a couple of snaps. This implies you can give lower inertness and a superior encounter for your clients at negligible expense.

7 Key Benefits Of Using AWS For Your Cloud Computing Needs

On account of the developing pattern for organizations to move their I.T. framework into the cloud, there are more alternatives for distributed computing administrations than at any time in recent memory.

The pattern doesn't seem to back off at any point in the near future; Moving to the cloud offers quick investment funds from the costly weight of owning and working servers.

As indicated by a study led by IDG Enterprise, cloud innovation is turning into a staple for associations, with 70% of big business organizations having in any event one application in the cloud. (2016 Cloud Computing Survey)

As referenced before, there are numerous alternatives accessible, however, as we would see it, none can contend with the pioneer of the general population cloud administration space, Amazon Web Services (AWS). Amazon tallies the absolute biggest associations on the planet as its clients: Adobe, Comcast, PBS, and Dow Jones (just to give some examples.)

We've assembled this rundown of seven advantages that your business can exploit when you use AWS to deal with your applications on the cloud.

7 Benefits Of Using AWS

1. Exhaustive

Changing from on-location stockpiling to the cloud is basic with AWS on account of the venture they have made in instruction and preparing. The cloud powerhouse offers an abundance of information on their site, including documentation and instructional exercises for beginning with AWS, their different administrations, and that's only the tip of the iceberg.

AWS likewise has a Partner Network, which is comprised of expert firms that help clients structure, designer, manufacture, move and deal with their outstanding tasks at hand and applications on AWS.

To acquire our counseling accomplice status Lofty Labs representatives passed a few accreditations and affirmations, had client references on AWS and demonstrated income through AWS administrations.

2. Practical

Regardless of whether you're a startup or huge undertaking organization you will spare by just utilizing the administrations your business needs at some random time. AWS has focused on estimating that it is a small amount of the cost that on-premises arrangements cost.

You can analyze the expense of running your applications in an on-premises or colocation condition to AWS with this convenient computing device.

3. Adaptable

Regardless of whether you're moving into the cloud just because, or relocating from another cloud administration, AWS has every one of the assets you have to upgrade your I.T.

framework. Their model backings scaling assets up or down, which implies your business doesn't need to stress when the limit is an issue or when necessities change.

4. Security

Verifying your business from potential information hacks and holes is a high need for AWS. They have some well-perceived consistence confirmations and stick to protection lAWS from around the globe.

Nasdaq, Dow Jones, and HealthCare.Gov all utilization AWS, which is a demonstration of how trusted AWS is as a safe cloud administration.

5. Improved Productivity

Having AWS bolster your distributed computing implies expelling the obligations and dangers related to lodging inward I.T. foundation. It additionally diminishes the requirement for I.T. bolster staff and spares your organization time and cash in the long haul.

6. Creative

There are articles that guarantee that it's Amazon's devotion to advancement, and not they're aggressive evaluating that at last prevails upon their clients. While confronting a valuing war with Microsoft and Google, Amazon still can't seem to confront rivalry in its devotion to creation, and experimentation. As per a participant of the last AWS reinvent Conference in 2016 AWS propelled almost 1000 new administrations a year ago.

7. Worldwide Leader

Amazon Web Services works in 190 nations and supports over a million dynamic clients. They check some of the biggest and littlest organizations on the planet as their clients and even help the open segment.

Advantages of Using AWS Cloud for Businesses

What is AWS Cloud and how might it advantage your business?

A portion of the advantages that organizations should think about utilizing the AWS cloud.

AWS, or Amazon Web Services, is an Amazon claimed distributed storage arrangement that displays a large group of advantages to entrepreneurs. AWS is portrayed by Amazon as "Offering an expansive arrangement of the worldwide register, stockpiling, database, examination, application, and sending administrations that assist associations with moving quicker, lower IT expenses, and scale applications." Here is a portion of the administrations offered by AWS and the business advantages of the AWS cloud.

Versatility

AWS offers benefits that are moderate for organizations everything being equal, from new companies to organizations with substantial traffic. One advantage of moving to AWS cloud is it can develop with your business. It can likewise help you develop by offering adaptability and web-based business and capacity arrangements that help bolster your business.

Duty-Free

One of the advantages of utilizing Amazon cloud administrations is that regardless of what AWS administration your business is that there's no dedication or agreement to get secured in and there no base spends to have the option to utilize their administrations. All server-based administrations are charged continuously, implying that whenever you end administration or capacity from a server, you're never again charged. This applies to organizations all sizes and is useful for any individual who's worried about overpaying for the capacity they don't require or being secured in an agreement with an item or administration that doesn't meet their requirements.

Security

AWS administrations offer improved and hearty security highlights, including:

Every minute of every day access to information specialists in the event that issues ought to emerge

Worked in the firewall, which takes into consideration unmistakable access, from profoundly prohibitive to open

IAM administrations that track clients get to

Multifaceted verification and scrambled information stockpiling abilities

Since information stockpiling and information security are so significant business, when changing to a cloud supplier or administration stockpiling supplier, it bodes well that security would be an exceptionally looked for after element and the AWS security is vigorous enough for most organizations.

Dependability

Amazon has an enormous reach and a monster group of tech specialists that has enabled them to fabricate a strong server arrange that has demonstrated to be reliable and steady. Most organizations report secure and dependable associations with information that help them to help and manufacture their business information foundations. This elite ability settles on AWS a decent decision for some organizations.

Adaptable and Customizable

AWS lets you select the programming language, working framework, database, and different resources, with the goal that you can make the arrangement that works best for your group. You're not secured in a new program that winds up costing your group time and cash as opposed to opening up assets to help proceed to develop and bolster your business. This sort of customization matched with the Amazon's trademark straightforwardness and easy to use stage is extremely alluring to certain organizations.

For what reason is AWS better? It gives a quick, adaptable, secure, and spending plan well-disposed answer for some, organizations searching for a distributed storage arrangement or application have. Numerous sellers profit by the AWS cloud and have utilized this simple to-utilize stage to help their business and IT needs. Has your business seen any advantages of AWS cloud administrations?? If not, have you at any point considered AWS or other cloud arrangements?

Prologue to Benefits of AWS

Amazon Web Services (AWS) is a stage for cloud benefits that are secure and offer administrations, for example, content conveyance, control calculation, database stockpiling, and so on. It helps in choosing the programming dialects, databases, working frameworks, application stages, and different administrations as indicated by the client's needs. These days, numerous organizations, for example, Nokia, Airbnb, Netflix, Slack, and Samsung are utilizing this stage for various business purposes due to its few points of interest. Let us investigate the advantages of AWS in the following area.

Advantages of AWS

Amazon Web Services gives an assortment of highlights that make it not quite the same as different firms. They are:

1. Portable Friendly Access

It incorporates two different ways AWS Mobile SDK and AWS Mobile Hub.

AWS Mobile SDK

AWS Mobile SDK underpins Android, React Native, IOS, Unity, Web, etc. With the assistance of this component, it is conceivable to get to various Amazon Web Services, for example, Lambda, DynamoDB and AWS S3 (Simple Storage Service).

AWS Mobile Hub

This Mobile Hub underpins you to get to a suitable and good component for your application. It is conceivable to create, test and screen the application utilizing the reassure, which is available in it. Some different highlights like message pop-up message and substance conveyance are additionally given by the AWS Mobile Hub.

2. Simple to Use

Contrasted with different stages, AWS gives an easy to use the stage in which an apprentice can likewise utilize it. It is conceivable in view of the unmistakable documentation and advantageous support AWS gives.

Well known Course in this class

Digital Week Sale

Distributed computing Training (18 Courses, 4+ Projects)

18 Online Courses | 4 Hands-on Projects | 100+ Hours | Verifiable Certificate of Completion | Lifetime Access

4.5 (2,360 ratings) Course Price

$39 $599

View Course

Related Courses

AWS Training (9 Courses, 3+ Projects)Azure Training (5 Courses, 4+ Projects)

3. Secure

Amazon Web Services gives a standard and secure framework where the client needs to pay just for the administrations they use. It gives a wide scope of administrations for security. Character Access and Management (IAM) is one such help where administrator oversees access to clients for utilizing AWS administrations. These days, Amazon Web Services presented instruments that survey security hazards naturally. It likewise furnishes apparatuses with encryption (both equipment and programming), Transport

Layer Security endorsements, protection from Distributed Denial of Service (DDoS) assaults, and channel of destructive traffic against applications. An apparatus known as Amazon Inspector is utilized to evaluate a client's Amazon Web Service cloud organization consequently so as to recognize security dangers and insufficiencies. Likewise, Amazon's private cloud encourages the client to make the occurrences private or open depending on their prerequisites.

4. Capacity

AWS gives high stockpiling, which can be utilized as free or combinational. The high stockpiling EC2 occasions can support the client on the off chance that they are utilizing any high Input/Output applications, for example, Hadoop, Data warehousing, and so forth.

Amazon gives various stockpiles, for example:

Amazon Elastic Block Store (EBS): Block level stockpiling that can be utilized alongside Elastic Compute Cloud (EC2) cases, which helps in keeping the information determined.

Amazon Glacier: Used primarily for long haul stockpiling where the information that isn't utilized habitually is put away. As it were capacity for information reinforcement and chronicle.

Amazon Simple Storage Service (S3): Helps in giving stockpiling through an electronic interface.

Amazon Elastic File System: This stockpiling is utilized for remaining burdens and applications that are available in people in general haze of Amazon Web Services.

Capacity Transport Devices: For business purposes, Amazon gives certain capacity gadgets, for example, Snowmobile and Snowball that can be shipped starting with one spot then onto the next. Snowmobile moves a lot of information by trucks that hold various hard drives so as to store petabytes of information. Snowball helps in moving information all through AWS with an expense of 1/fifth not as much as that of moving through the web.

5. Pay Per Use

In contrast to different stages, Amazon web administrations don't make the client pay for every one of the administrations that are available on the stage. It charges the client just for the assets, stockpiling, and the data transfer capacity they are utilizing. Thinking about this reality, it is the most significant component of business segments drawing in AWS contrasted with different ones.

6. Multi-Region Backups

Amazon gives a few districts where the client can keep their information and cases. These districts incorporate accessibility zones that are protected from disappointment in some other zones. The primary motivation behind Multi-Region Backups is to dispatch the EC2 cases in any area so as to ensure the client's applications. On the off chance that the zones are in a similar area, organize dormancy and cost will be low. Locales can be in independent geographic territories, provinces, and so on. Clients can pick the area as indicated by their accommodation. Furthermore, a help Cloud Ranger (outsider assistance) consequently reinforcements the information in various districts.

7. Unwavering Quality and Scalability

Amazon offers a framework that scales depending on the utilization. Because of this, the expense of utilization can be low if the client downsizes the examples that are utilizing. It is as of now referenced under the element 'pay per use'. Versatility highlight has become the best answer for enormous organizations since they needn't bother with any extra assets on the off chance that they are coming up short on capacity.

8. Databases

There are a few databases Amazon offers, which are overseen by them itself. Some of them appear in the table underneath.

Kind of Database Applications, AWS administration

Document User profiling, Content management, Amazon DocumentDB

Key-Value Gaming applications, Web applications of high traffic, Amazon DynamoDB

Relational Traditional, ERP, E-Commerce Amazon Redshift, Amazon Aurora, Amazon Relational Database Service (RDS)

Graph Recommendation Engine, Fraud detection Amazon Neptune

Ledger Banking exchanges, supply chains Amazon Quantum Ledger Database (QLDB)

In-MemoryGeospatial applications, Caching, game pioneer boards Amazon ElastiCache for Redis, Amazon ElastiCache for Memcached

Time Series Industrial telemetry, IoT, DevOps Amazon Timestream

9. The Executives and Monitoring

To oversee and screen, Admin, can perform undertakings, for example,

Track the asset and application wellbeing, cloud asset arrangement

Mechanize foundation design

Hold client exercises

All these are finished with the assistance of specific apparatuses.

3 Benefits of Amazon EC2 Virtual Server Hosting

Amazon Elastic Compute Cloud (Amazon EC2) is a center segment of Amazon Web Services. It enables clients to lease virtual PCs to run PC applications, as a virtual private server. Virtual private servers are fundamentally the same as in usefulness to devoted physical servers. Be that as it may, they are more cost proficient and can be booted in minutes instead of obtaining, introduce, and send a physical server rack.

A virtual private server runs its own duplicate of a working framework, has endeavor level security controls, and gives clients complete access and control. EC2 furnishes clients with versatile, on-request register and handling power for organizations all things considered.

Here are 3 one of a kind advantages of Amazon EC2 and why organizations can profit by using Amazon's virtual server facilitating stage:

Unlimited authority easily of Access

Clients have total regulatory authority over their virtual servers (otherwise called figure occasions) with Amazon EC2. Basically, Amazon EC2 gives a similar degree of access and control as a physical server worked locally in the workplace. Figure occurrences are effectively overseen through the Amazon EC2 web interface, which enables clients to scale up or down, boot examples, and arrange processor settings with a couple of snaps of a mouse.

Also, virtual servers on EC2 can be overseen consequently by means of an application program interface (API) that can be set up by downloading a product improvement pack

(SDK) from AWS in a decision of programming dialects.

Capacity to Select a Platform of Your Choice

At the point when you dispatch an occasion in EC2, you get the capacity to run a working arrangement of your decision. Clients can choose from numerous Linux circulations or they can run Microsoft Windows Server. This is a significant component for most organizations, particularly for those thinking about doing a change to the cloud.

In the event that an organization has utilized Windows Server for quite a long time and has fabricated applications, databases, and capacity units inside the Windows Server structure, they shouldn't need to reconstruct their IT foundation in the cloud to run on an alternate stage. As clients can choose their preferred working arrangement, moving to an

EC2 example is cultivated considerably more effectively.

Secure

EC2 has numerous worked in security highlights. At the point when you dispatch a case, it is run in a virtual private cloud that is a coherently disconnected system. Clients have full oversight over who can get to the occasions in the cloud. Amazon EC2 has security bunches that go about as virtual firewalls to control traffic to one or numerous examples. Clients can set up rules for every security gathering and adjust rules whenever.

On the off chance that an organization chooses to keep a few procedures running on reason and they need to interface their virtual private mists to the physical equipment on location, they can set up a consistent association through an equipment VPN gadget.

Searching for help with propelling your first Amazon EC2 example? Privo IT can furnish you with the master's direction and help with propelling cloud cases through Amazon Web Services and Amazon EC2. Connect for a free meeting!

Top 9 advantages of AWS preparing

For distributed computing information, Amazon Web Services or AWS is without a doubt a difficult course for everybody. Because of its center consistency with distributed computing, it gives the correct stage to experience difficulties in the business field. It is working for more than huge years to convey a careful answer to get together a three inline cloud specialist co-op. Obviously, it is guaranteed to find the correct assistance and hold income on the cloud piece of the overall industry.

While going to AWS instructional class, it utilizes each changing principles to approve information on experts. It satisfies up for industry guidelines guaranteed with consolidated patterns. By and large, patterns are continually changing quickly due it is sure AWS Certification Benefits.

One should snatch the advantages related with going to this confirmation regarding the accompanying level of accreditation. It at that point oversaw by controlling with intrigue and means nature of the activity for tentative arrangements. Along these lines, it thinks about information in the related business area and ready to work with a cloud specialist co-op.

The AWS accreditation, then again, uncovers numerous advantages while going to an instructional class. It gets proficient and you can secure numerous advantages by using the accreditation.

Enquiry Now

Fields set apart with a * are required

Name *

Email *

Telephone *

Remark/Course name

1. Addition better pay

While picking up information in the AWS field, it gets a great salary, which essentially supports your compensation. On the off chance that you are searching for a splendid affirmation, do AWS course that certainly gives you certainty and increment your compensation. It gives edge installment, which is conceivable to refresh with more things and the requirement for installment.

This radically causes one to increase better results by refreshing more open doors throughout your life.

2. Distributed computing is what's to come

Distributed computing is something that will harvest more profession prospects in the coming years. Nowadays, organizations are putting resources into a high in the distributed computing arrangements. This is the explanation that has offered ascend to the AWS confirmation necessity. It's the best time for the experts to get prepared on AWS and secure their future.

3. A positive effect on continue

With an AWS instructional class accreditation, you can add some energy to your resume. Most organizations incline toward workers owing to an AWS confirmation. You can get a need with the selection of accreditation on your resume and can anticipate incredible possibilities.

4. Achieve more openings for work

While finishing the AWS confirmation, you will get more business open doors towards moving the cloud. There will be more open doors thumping the entryway with the goal that you will get a splendid vocation according to the authentication approval. It is taking a shot at AWS ventures than there will be a remote possibility of picking up AWS accreditation according to the necessities.

In the event that you are searching for work in an organization, you ought to get AWS confirmation until the end of time. There is an interest confirmation from up-and-comers so it ought to acquire a more opening for work for all. In this way, it must experience a well-arranged affirmation appropriate for increasing more open doors at any rate.

5. Advantages for specialist and manager

Aside from understudies, the AWS confirmation course is enormously useful for specialists and representatives. It gives the greatest possibility so it could ready to recognize enough working involvement in AWS preparing. It incorporates advanced groups so you will stay an expert competitor subsequent to finishing the course. This without a doubt causes specialist possibility to partake in huge undertakings by having confirmation.

In the event that you are searching for online assets, it should manual to give identifications according to the choice. Most organizations are refreshing with the correct abilities for going to AWS preparing reasonable for your future objectives. It should pick up the certainty of customers in getting AWS ventures.

6. Incorporates future improvement

From the start, Cloud registering innovation has achieved a standard job in making legitimate difficulties in late business segments. This ought to experience by thinking about further improvement by taking care of numerous organizations as quickly as time permits. The advantages of learning AWS fledge server farm by running everything dependent on the distributed computing recipe.

It is reasonable for each office and innovation uncovers the accomplishment in distributed computing in the server farm. The affirmation preparing offers essential information in conveying secure and modest access to the cloud. This is the most compelling motivation that one ought to experience preparing of AWS and getting crisp alumni to verify your future objectives.

7. The requirement for master direction

At whatever point there are favorable circumstances of AWS affirmation close by, it is an incredible open door for everybody who needs to become ace in it. There is a gigantic interest for talented experts who can take a shot at AWS. The AWS affirmation preparing is continually giving hundreds or thousands of businesses to incorporate with fruitful tasks.

You will discover openings in almost 600 government associations. Also, organizations give arrangements, which are in thousands and oversee it by taking by and large AWS confirmation preparing. It causes most designers to prevail invocation and ready to acknowledge complex demands identified with the AWS course. Along these lines, become proficient in AWS and set your future for good advancement.

8. Add to your resume

An AWS affirmation is continually giving the best chance to refresh it to your resume. It should arrive at the meeting table by getting it as per the organization's direction. In this way, it gives great updation to your resume by designing with the correct obstructions in the resume update. It is indispensable for positions identified with the AWS affirmation esteem.

In this way, one must go to the instructional class to get into splendid future objectives. It is constantly required to get it dependent on the administrator posts and reasonable for adding to your resume. It gives a great opening to work for everybody who finished the AWS course.

9. A great number of chances

AWS instructional class increases current standards for you while you are going after a position. With the affirmation close by, your odds to pick up work rise.

Aside from the above reasons, the activity showcase in the field of AWS has risen enormously. Contrasted with the year 2017, it had been normal that the coming year will bring an ascent of about 45%, for example, more openings for work and a superior compensation scale for AWS confirmed experts.

At the point when such incredible magnificent outcomes are normal, you can invest your cash and energy in AWS affirmation. It is justified, despite all the trouble in the present progressively moving the world.

CHAPTER 6

AWS Networking

Virtual Network Design

In what capacity would it be a good idea for me to structure my Amazon Virtual Private Cloud (VPC)?

This brief gives significant level prescribed procedures to structuring an Amazon VPC system and layouts the most widely recognized single-VPC arrangements. It likewise offers direction on the most proficient method to estimate your VPC and subnets. For more subtleties »

By what method would it be a good idea for me to execute exceptionally accessible remote associations with AWS from a solitary server farm?

This brief depicts basic designs and contemplations for making profoundly accessible VPN and AWS Direct Connect associations between Amazon VPC and a solitary server farm. For more subtleties »

In what capacity would it be a good idea for me to actualize exceptionally accessible remote associations with AWS from numerous server farms?

This brief portrays basic designs and contemplations for making exceptionally accessible VPN and AWS Direct Connect associations between Amazon VPC and numerous server farms, including steering guidance for enhancing system way determination in complex system conditions. For more subtleties »

Remote Connectivity

How would I associate different VPCs in a solitary AWS Region?

This brief depicts AWS prescribed methodologies for making private associations between Amazon VPC arranges in a similar locale utilizing VPC peering, AWS Direct Connect, or a VPC committed to transitive steering. For more subtleties »

How would I associate various VPCs in various AWS Regions?

This brief portrays prescribed methodologies for making private associations between AWS locales by directing over AWS or non-AWS systems relying upon a client's utilization case and necessities. For more subtleties »

How would I share a solitary VPN association with different VPCs?

AWS clients with various Amazon VPC arranges frequently need to limit the number of remote associations with AWS. This short tends to key contemplations, suggestions, and normal methodologies for interfacing various

Amazon VPC systems to on-premises framework utilizing a solitary VPN association. For more subtleties »

How would I manufacture a worldwide trip organize on AWS?

Figure out how to make a worldwide travel center point on the AWS Cloud. This answer gives structural direction, organizing best practices, and prescriptive AWS arrangements utilizing Aviatrix and Cisco items. For more subtleties »

How would I actualize network to my VPC over MPLS?

AWS clients who use Multiprotocol Label Switching (MPLS) to interface topographically scattered organization arranges regularly need to join this availability into their general system structure. This brief portrays normal arrangements for making profoundly accessible, productive associations among

AWS and an MPLS organize. For more subtleties »

How would I execute VPN observing on AWS?

Observing is a significant piece of keeping up the unwavering quality, accessibility, and execution of your VPN associations. This website page gives direction to help make a checking plan and computerized and manual devices for observing your VPN associations. For more subtleties »

System Security

How would I execute VPC departure controls?

This short tends to key contemplations and suggestions for overseeing outbound (departure) traffic from Amazon VPC systems. It portrays Amazon VPC highlights for controlling departure traffic and different choices including outsider contributions that fuse extra sifting, observing, and traffic-control capacities. For more subtleties »

What the executives and observing highlights are accessible for Amazon VPC?

This concise gives an outline of the AWS administrations and highlights that clients can use to control access to their system assets and to screen organize traffic and arrangement changes. It likewise incorporates suggestions for outsider items that give the extra system the executives and observing abilities. For more subtleties »

How would I shield my applications from DDoS assaults?

In the occasion of a Distributed Denial of Service (DDoS) assault, AWS clients can use numerous abilities to ingest and divert undesirable traffic while working with AWS backing to alleviate the issue. This brief gives general prescribed procedures to DDoS security, distinguishes key AWS administrations for moderating DDoS assaults, and depicts elevated level assault alleviation approaches for normal application designs. For more subtleties »

What organize security highlights are accessible for Amazon VPC?

AWS and AWS Partner Network individuals offer an exhaustive arrangement of abilities to assist clients with verifying their Amazon VPC systems. This brief gives a diagram of these capacities, featuring highlights for arranging traffic control, directing, and firewalls, and furthermore incorporates generally accepted procedures for organizing security. For more subtleties »

How would I execute VPC remote clients get to controls?

A significant safety effort is to successfully control remote client access to assets in your Amazon VPC to recognize approved and unapproved clients. This brief gives AWS clients best practices and regular methodologies for picking a remote access arrangement as a feature of a comprehensive system security methodology.

Virtual Network Design

In what capacity would it be a good idea for me to structure my Amazon Virtual Private Cloud (VPC)?

This brief gives significant level prescribed procedures to structuring an Amazon VPC system and layouts the most widely recognized single-VPC arrangements. It likewise offers direction on the most proficient method to estimate your VPC and subnets. For more subtleties »

By what method would it be a good idea for me to execute exceptionally accessible remote associations with AWS from a solitary server farm?

This brief depicts basic designs and contemplations for making profoundly accessible VPN and AWS Direct Connect associations between Amazon VPC and a solitary server farm. For more subtleties »

In what capacity would it be a good idea for me to actualize exceptionally accessible remote associations with AWS from numerous server farms?

This brief portrays basic designs and contemplations for making exceptionally accessible VPN and AWS Direct Connect associations between Amazon VPC and numerous server farms, including steering guidance for enhancing system way determination in complex system conditions. For more subtleties »

Remote Connectivity

How would I associate different VPCs in a solitary AWS Region?

This brief depicts AWS prescribed methodologies for making private associations between Amazon VPC arranges in a similar locale utilizing VPC peering, AWS Direct Connect, or a VPC committed to transitive steering. For more subtleties »

How would I associate various VPCs in various AWS Regions?

This brief portrays prescribed methodologies for making private associations between AWS locales by directing over AWS or non-AWS systems relying upon a client's utilization case and necessities. For more subtleties »

How would I share a solitary VPN association with different VPCs?

AWS clients with various Amazon VPC arranges frequently need to limit the number of remote associations with AWS. This short tends to key contemplations, suggestions, and normal methodologies for interfacing various Amazon VPC systems to on-premises framework utilizing a solitary VPN association. For more subtleties »

How would I manufacture a worldwide trip organize on AWS?

Figure out how to make a worldwide travel center point on the AWS Cloud. This answer gives structural direction, organizing best practices, and prescriptive AWS arrangements utilizing Aviatrix and Cisco items. For more subtleties »

How would I actualize network to my VPC over MPLS?

AWS clients who use Multiprotocol Label Switching (MPLS) to interface topographically scattered organization arranges regularly need to join this availability into their general system structure. This brief portrays normal arrangements for making profoundly accessible, productive associations among AWS and an MPLS organize. For more subtleties »

How would I execute VPN observing on AWS?

Observing is a significant piece of keeping up the unwavering quality, accessibility, and execution of your VPN associations. This website page gives direction to help make a checking plan and computerized and manual devices for observing your VPN associations. For more subtleties »

System Security

How would I execute VPC departure controls?

This short tends to key contemplations and suggestions for overseeing outbound (departure) traffic from Amazon VPC systems. It portrays Amazon VPC highlights for controlling departure traffic and different choices including outsider contributions that fuse extra sifting, observing, and traffic-control capacities. For more subtleties »

What the executives and observing highlights are accessible for Amazon VPC?

This concise gives an outline of the AWS administrations and highlights that clients can use to control access to their system assets and to screen organize traffic and arrangement changes. It likewise incorporates suggestions for outsider items that give the extra system the executives and observing abilities. For more subtleties »

How would I shield my applications from DDoS assaults?

In the occasion of a Distributed Denial of Service (DDoS) assault, AWS clients can use numerous abilities to ingest and divert undesirable traffic while working with AWS backing to alleviate the issue. This brief gives general prescribed procedures to DDoS security, distinguishes key AWS administrations for moderating DDoS assaults, and depicts elevated level assault alleviation approaches for normal application designs. For more subtleties »

What organize security highlights are accessible for Amazon VPC?

AWS and AWS Partner Network individuals offer an exhaustive arrangement of abilities to assist clients with verifying their Amazon VPC systems. This brief gives a diagram of these capacities, featuring highlights for arranging traffic control, directing, and firewalls, and furthermore incorporates generally accepted procedures for organizing security. For more subtleties »

How would I execute VPC remote clients get to controls?

A significant safety effort is to successfully control remote client access to assets in your Amazon VPC to recognize approved and unapproved clients. This brief gives AWS clients best practices and regular methodologies for picking a remote access arrangement as a feature of a comprehensive system security methodology. For more subtleties »

CHAPTER 7

Development Services For Website Owners

Website composition And Development Services: The 5 Your Business Really Needs

In this way, you're considering building (or refreshing) your business site.

Congrats! That is an incredible move for your business. Crosswise over businesses, sites are one of the top wellsprings of traffic and deals. Accordingly, making an interest in an online nearness is a top-level business decision!

On the web, there are unlimited choices for building a business site including DIY stages and here now gone again later designers. However, on the off chance that you need to construct a webpage that will get you the most value for your money and truly make a living, you have to put resources into business website architecture and advancement administrations.

Obviously, such as whatever else that merits the speculation, decisions for website composition and advancement administrations run the array from one-time conferences to undeniable bundles.

To enable you to choose what sorts of website architecture and improvement benefit your business REALLY needs, here are the 5 we prescribe.

1. Web Strategy

Everything great beginnings with a methodology. Also, with regards to building a business site, web procedure is a web improvement administration that will assist you with going the additional mile.

Essentially, a web technology is utilized to characterize a reason for your site.

It mulls over both the requirements of the business and the necessities of the client to make a completely utilitarian online experience. It likewise characterizes objectives for transient achievement and long haul development to guarantee a site keeps on filling its proposed need long after it's underlying execution.

Without web technique, it's possible your private company site will simply wind up another URL without a reason on the overall web. It may sound brutal, yet that is the reason web procedure is a fundamental web advancement administration for independent companies.

To make a web technique for your business site, we suggest working with a web designer.

Proficient web advancement groups can create the best web systems since they know the intricate details of the web, inclinations of clients and the complexities of a site.

Also, if the procedure doesn't appear to be working, they realize what updates to start to make it right.

2. Facilitating, Back-up, and Security

When you have an extraordinary system set up for your site, it's a great opportunity to dive in and start building! Be that as it may, pause... not before you source a site have, site back-up and site security.

Here's the reason.

Host: A site has is a home for your site. Without a host, it is difficult to get to your business' online nearness.

Back-up: It takes a great deal of work to construct a site (and here and there a ton of cash), and you don't need that to go to squander! By ensuring your site is supported up, you help to ensure that you will never lose relevant data that could represent the moment of truth in your business.

Security: Everyone realizes that information ruptures are a genuine risk in this day and age. Also, on the off chance that you have a business site, the one thing you need to make certain of is that you don't turn into the casualty of one. Putting resources into site security will help make that conceivable.

On the off chance that you work with a web engineer to make your site, they will have the option to supply you with the best alternatives for facilitating, back-up, and security access.

They realize which organizations to trust and which have demonstrated track records for progress. Furthermore, what's more than that, they will have the option to deal with the facilitating, back-up and security, so you don't need to!

3. Website Composition

How your site looks have any kind of effect in its exhibition. Consequently, it's certainly astute to put resources into proficient website architecture when fabricating a webpage for your private venture.

Website composition incorporates picking the best possible WordPress topic, modules and extra highlights for your webpage. It characterizes how your site looks and how your business is seen by your crowd. Be that as it may, TRUE website composition is considerably more than only an alluring outward appearance. It likewise incorporates site responsiveness and usefulness.

Versatile visits represent about half of visits for all sites.

Along these lines, you need to ensure your independent venture site looks great from both a work area and a versatile viewpoint. Responsive website architecture administrations are what make that conceivable via naturally resizing and reshaping the highlights of your site to fit the portable screen it needs to show up on.

Web engineers who have some expertise in website architecture will have the option to take the vision you have for your site and transform it into a reality by picking the topic that is best for you.

Gifted website specialists are even ready to work out custom subjects intended to address the entirety of your issues thus that there will never be an issue with your site you can't fix.

4. Site Layouts

Have you at any point visited a site wanting to discover basic data just to find that you can't get a handle on where anything could or ought to be found?

In the event that you have, you know it's the most noticeably terrible. On the off chance that you haven't, you're fortunate.

At the point when you manufacture a site for your business, you need to guarantee site guests don't have that experience and can get to the data they need rapidly.

Webpage format website composition administrations make this a reality by deliberately putting invitations to take action, routes, and connections over your site where guests will make certain to see them.

In the event that you work with a web designer to make a webpage format, they will have the option to supply you with a wide range of alternatives to browse. In like manner, they will have the option to prescribe what format they accept will work best for your group of spectators, or even make a custom design explicitly customized to address your issues.

5. Website Improvement

At last, the three enchantment expressions of the overall web – Search Engine Optimization (SEO). In the event that there's anything worth putting resources into, it's this without a doubt!

Web optimization is the thing that takes your site from simply one more URL to an outcome in Google look through that gets snaps and leads.

Behind great SEO there's a ton of research, plan advancement, usage, progress following, and alterations. On the off chance that you attempt to put resources into these web improvement administrations, you're going to profit incredibly.

Notwithstanding, on the off chance that you go into your site without an arrangement for SEO or an approach to oversee it, it's almost certain you won't get the outcomes you need.

Commonly, SEO web improvement administrations incorporate a review to see where you as of now remain with SEO, a rundown of what watchwords and expressions to use on your webpage and a technique to rebuild the substance on your site and make all the more so you can progress in the web crawler positions.

6. Maintenance

OK, we realize we said 5; however, this one is a reward! In case you will put resources into ANY of the website architecture and advancement administrations we discussed above, you need to put resources into site upkeep too!

As you assemble a site, you will see that it is anything, but a one and done process. Rather, it's an undertaking that takes standard consideration and consideration.

What's more, regularly, the consideration and consideration sites require is a lot for entrepreneurs to deal with (after everything you DO have a ton on your plate).

Putting resources into site support as a component of your website composition and advancement administration bundle will put your brain very still since you'll realize that everything is all around dealt with and in great hands.

CHAPTER 8

AWS Computer

Lately, web improvement re-appropriating is the pattern. This is on the grounds that the majority of the organizations transform into online today. Clients need to get their required help on the web. That is the reason more quantities of organizations start their administrations on the web. The explanation is online administrations give a lot of points of interest and advantages to the organizations.

The site is the best method for e-promoting and this makes organizations to make a site for them. Giving administrations through a site is an insightful method to drive more clients to the business.

Web Development Services in India

This is impossible for the organization itself. Along these lines, the organization must need the assistance of web improvement organizations. Web Development Company in India offers a broad scope of web advancement administrations to various organizations. They assemble sites for organizations and organizations with more current aptitudes, devices and with ability. Organizations that need to build up their business economically can go for this sort of web administrations and they unquestionably get more advantages from this.

Purposes Behind Picking A Web Improvement Organization

There are various reasons are there for picking a web improvement organization

Efficient

Relegating the undertaking of site assembling and keeping up web administrations to an organization, spare a great deal of time. This is on the grounds that there is more information is should have been scholarly for building up a site or web administration.

Website Streamlining

This is one of the most significant highlights gave by web advancement organizations. This causes organizations to make their site top positioned among the top web indexes. The site designers have these instruments that help your site to be unmistakable in the web index. This will drive more clients to the business.

Site Similarity

A decent site ought to be perfect with all programs. An organization can make this with the assistance of these organizations. Web designers can make a webpage perfect with all the internet browsers. In this way the organization's webpage load on all internet browsers

Intensity

You ought to be in front of your business rivals on all stages. The site ought to be speaking to the eye of the client just as simple to utilize. By enlisting a decent web organization this will be anything, but difficult to accomplish.

Most Ideal Ways to Choose Web Design and Development Services

A site is the reflection of your business. An innovative site can truly be a magnet to draw in potential clients on your site. Each client enlists a remarkable site.

For this, your landing page configuration must be truly attractive and alluring. Search for web advancement benefits that have made the best landing page structures for their customers.

There are many web improvement organizations in the computerized promoting space. Everyone will pitch their customers with administrations that are superior to other people.

You need to utilize your very own watchfulness with regards to picking the best website architecture and advancement administrations for your business. This is the genuine 'represent the deciding moment' for you.

Here Are Some Points To Keep In Mind While Choosing Your Web Design And Development Services

Website architecture And Development Services

Fix Your Budget Before Opting For Any Web Development Services

Contingent upon the achievement and believability of the organization, distinctive website architecture and advancement administrations organizations will provide diverse cost estimates. Some will show you the sort of work they have done in making the best landing page structures.

Web Development Services

Some will show you the inventive sites that they have made. Some will show the traffic that their colleague has created on the site, etc. It is anything, but difficult to become overly energetic with this. The most ideal approach to begin the assessment of a website architecture accomplice is to fix your spending first.

Utilize your spending limit as a channel to make a pool of organizations that can offer your administrations inside your financial limit. Work in some adaptability on the spending limit and keep some extension for exchange.

Request Quotations For Best Homepage Design

Approach your advanced promoting accomplice for citations or go for select web improvement administrations supplier. You could likewise assess both of these.

Best Homepage Design

The majority of the offices don't distribute their timings on their site. You need to set up a gathering with the organization for extricating this data.

Set Your Expectations Straight While Asking For Web Design And Development Services

When your spending limit is fixed and the citations are in, right now is an ideal opportunity to get ready for the gathering. While meeting diverse website architecture and improvement administrations organizations, keep a plan for your gathering.

Website composition And Development Services

This would incorporate the scope of administrations offered (content, reconciliations, landing page plans). In the event that you need an innovative site, pour in your underlying contemplations. Request that the organization return with their musings on it.

Approach them for every concealed expense and charges. It is ideal to explain the evaluated receipt sum in the main gathering itself. This straightforwardness is significant for taking issues to the following level.

Request Projects Handled By That Web Development Company

All website composition and improvement organizations will have a rundown of past customers. This will be extremely useful for you to comprehend the sort of work that will be conveyed to you.

Web Development Company

At the point when you start your pursuit, check the landing page structures of your rival organizations. Additionally, make a note of the intriguing sites you run over.

You could go through these two sources to accompany the best landing page structure for your business. Match the skill of the organization that you are assessing premise the desires that you have.

Request Client Retention Rate Before Selecting Any Web Development Services

Customer Retention Rates are demonstrative of consumer loyalty. A customer standard for the dependability of 90% or above demonstrates the polished skill of these organizations. A site isn't something that any business would change intermittently.

Imaginative Site

When you make an imaginative site, you would just need minor changes or upgradations to be done on it. This turns into a piece of website architecture and advancement administrations offered by the organization.

Customer Retention Rates of 60-70% isn't acceptable. Be on a post for the best organization in your financial limit.

Request Single Point Of Contact For Your Web Development Project
Building up an innovative site for your business is a significant undertaking. The

entirety of the other advanced advertising roads opens up once your site is prepared.

Web Development Project

Forgoing hard and fast in publicizing your organization and producing deals through your site, you need the site to be proficient. Landing page structure, a list of items and administrations, installment portals and so on structure an indispensable piece of your site.

For the creation and the executives of your site, request a solitary purpose of contact from your web improvement administration supplier. This works in proprietorship and obligation. You additionally evade pointless subsequent meet-ups later on.

Set Up A Plan About Your Requirements Which You Need Form The Web Design And Development Services Team

The greater part of the website architecture and advancement benefits additionally offer computerized advertising administrations. At the point when you approach the organization for your needs, set up a stage by stage plan.

Website composition And Development Services

The arrangement can be examined with a practical desire setting. On the off chance that your website composition accomplice comprehends that you are searching for a long haul affiliation, they will likewise offer more advantages. Check for client care contacts and audits of the office on the web.

Request Creative Website Updations In Your Plan

There are website architecture and advancement benefits that give you instruments to make changes in your site. You can likewise post, alter or erase content from your site.

Innovative Websites

Some different organizations don't give this entrance and do the updates for you. Check this viewpoint when you pick the best web improvement organization. On the off chance that you have an in-house master to deal with your site, at that point request the entrance.

Something else, request a dependable venture administrator to address your needs instantly. It is ideal to explain this perspective to stay away from inconvenience later on.

Check For Relocation Services From The Website Development Company

Once in a while, your current facilitating administration and your website architecture office may not be good. Some website composition and advancement administration organizations have your site themselves.

Site Development Company

They may likewise switch facilitating to another restrictive supplier. In either case, you must know about what is happening on your site. Banding together with geologically good website architecture and advancement administrations organization works best for your business.

Some enormous organizations with a worldwide nearness may appear to be alluring. It is, nonetheless, best to comprehend their movement administrations and customers who are utilizing these.

Be Deadline Driven With Your Website Creation Services Team

Many website architecture and improvement organizations take on work yet don't have the transfer speed for it. At the point when you pick your accomplice, make an arrangement with solid cutoff times. Request landing page configuration to be done first.

Site Creation Services

When this is affirmed, different parts of causing an inventive site can be taken up. In the event that your accomplice stays in front of the calendar that you have set, you can be guaranteed that you have picked the correct accomplice.

Being explicit about your objectives takes out superfluous work. It likewise makes working in cooperation simpler. Cutoff times have a demonstrated reputation for driving efficiencies. Use it to further your potential benefit.

Many website architecture and advancement administrations are incredibly proficient in their work. Be that as it may, there are others likewise who are amateurs and may provide a lower cost estimate, however, not convey according to desires.

Taking verbal criticism from peers is likewise significant. In the event that you have business friends or companions who are entrepreneurs, do take their input on the website architecture and advancement organizations that they have collaborated with.

The Best Web Development Services For Your Business

The idea of eCommerce is developing in fame among different kinds of organizations. This has brought about an expanding number of online stores. Because of the rising challenge in business and the developing requests of customers, the improvement of a web-based business site has become a productive and incredible methodology in organizations around the world.

In such a manner, on the off chance that you are an entrepreneur who is intending to have your very own site fabricated, at that point, it is suggested that you utilize proficient web advancement administrations. Just an expert web application improvement organization is equipped for giving you an alluring, successful, and proficient looking site.

Web Development Miami – Types of Web Application Development Services

Your site is frequently the early introduction that individuals get about your business. It is then significant for your site to look engaging and for its functionalities to be working appropriately. It needs to make your guests feel good before they can think about making a buy.

The whole web advancement process includes organizing security arrangements, customer-side/server-side scripting, web content improvement, and website architecture. In such a manner, coming up next is a portion of the web application advancement benefits that you can profit from when you utilize the expert web improvement administrations of an organization for programming improvement Miami.

Here are some of the Web Application Development Services:

Web Development

Web advancement administrations include the formation of a site for your business. It empowers the site to work as per the site proprietor's necessities. It relates to the non-structure parts of web improvement and includes the composition of markup and coding.

Administrations in web improvement Miami extend from the making of website pages with plain content to complex electronic business applications, interpersonal organization applications, and Web-based applications. Coming up next is the chain of importance for web improvement: 1.) Client-side scripting; 2.) Server-side scripting; and 3.) Database innovation.

Website Architecture

The website architecture incorporates the manner in which the site works, the manner in which it looks, and its substance. It is a procedure that includes the conceptualization, arranging, and working of a gathering of electronic documents that decide the pictures, designs, structure, content styles, hues, and format of the website pages.

It likewise incorporates the intelligent highlights that decide how your webpage's guests see the site. There are many web improvement instruments for structuring a site, however, on the off chance that you are inexperienced with them or on the off chance that you need an expert to take a shot at it, at that point, you can utilize benefits in programming advancement Miami. With the aptitude of expert improvement administrations, you can make certain of your clients' fulfillment since the website composition can address their issues.

With a well-planned site, the guests can rapidly discover what they need to know without pointless perplexity. The web advancement experts will guarantee that the website composition is steady, unsurprising, and can be effectively comprehended. This at that point manufactures and cultivates a positive association with the clients.

Additionally, an all-around planned site drAWS in web indexes. Your site must be coded in a way that web indexes can peruse. A well-planned site likewise keeps away from specialized glitches, which can dismiss a client. A portion of these glitches incorporate dropped pictures, broken connections, and protracted stacking times.

Web Improvement Administrations

Installment Gateway Integration

An installment door empowers you to acknowledge online installments through your site. In that capacity your trader account must be incorporated with online passage processors, for example, PayPal, Skrill, Payoneer, Google Checkout, and YouPay among others.

Database Development

A site that sudden spikes in demand for a database application improvement stage enable you to include, change, and update content on your site in a powerful way. The database can store a lot of data and can be effectively kept up. It can likewise interface with the site's front-end.

Database-driven sites are required in intuitive sites, for example, vehicle postings, land postings, online stores, and blogging sites among others. In such a manner, an organization that gives benefits in programming improvement Miami will incorporate the database with the site's back-end stage so it can associate with the client.

Back-end Administration Platform

Also called the site's back-end, the back-end organization arranges enables you to control every element of your site with exceptionally insignificant exertion, enabling you to save money on costs. This empowers you to keep up your very own site without procuring a website admin. Suppliers of administrations on web advancement Miami can assemble this stage based on your needs.

They can likewise make and give all the code no duplicates and with no security issues. They will treat the entirety of your data, for example, your own data, passwords, charge card data, and others with care so as to maintain a strategic distance from any security rupture. The back-end organization stage is perfect with a wide range of online administrations.

Site Maintenance

When the site is ready for action, the subsequent stage is to keep the site refreshed and new. In such a manner, you can likewise ask your web improvement supplier to support your site and downplay the expense. It is important to keep your site kept up with the goal that you can be educated regarding the conceivable outcomes and possess satisfactory the energy for arranging your online methodologies and for maintaining the attention on guaranteeing that you make a benefit.

Online Application Development

Online application improvement administrations are another web administration that you might need to exploit so as to advance your business. This basically implies putting your product application on the Internet as opposed to having it introduced on the client's PC. Along these lines, clients worldwide will have the option to get to your application.

Web-based Business and Shopping Baskets

Web-based business and shopping baskets empower you to sell your items anyplace on the planet. It will develop your clients and increment your benefits. An internet shopping basket is a gathering of programming that can be utilized to make an eCommerce site or an online customer-facing facade. It fills in as a virtual shopping basket that anyone with a PC can get to. It empowers clients to pick the item that they need to purchase with only a tick.

It likewise enables them to make their buy on the web. At the point when you utilize the administrations of a web application improvement organization, they can without much of a stretch remember this element for your site, as they utilize advanced web advancement devices.

Top Web Development Companies in 2017 I am alluding to a portion of the Top web advancement organizations of 2017 with proficient web designers in the accompanying beneath the list. By Sarah Maxwell thirteenth Nov 2017 +0 Website-a multi-practical specialized instrument for your association or business. A decent site helps in pulling in clients online that fabricates a solid connection among you and your client.

Be that as it may, each fruitful business needs an expert site advancement, which is the best method for building up your image on the web and in keeping your business aggressive. Web Development Services " alt=" Web Development Services "/> Website Development has come up far from its static variant to a dynamic one. Today, site proprietors are attempting to satisfy the expanding need of the guests by improving and actualizing a few mechanized functionalities. In that capacity, the web improvement process is accepting unmistakable quality step by step and these days a basic site has taken the state of a custom web application by strategic and specialized up degrees. Structuring and building up a site is a significant advance to dispatch your business with the web nearness. Getting a site created and facilitated on the World Wide Web is loaded with endless little and huge advances and stages.

So one must be cautious while picking the correct web improvement organization for their site. Keeping the fierce changes occurring in the present innovation world in context, I am alluding to a portion of the top web advancement organizations of 2017 with proficient web engineers in the accompanying underneath list. Rundown of Top Web Development Companies in 2017 Tvisha

Technologies: Tvisha-a powerhouse site improvement organization, who upgrade the general population picture of your business by expertly setting up and planning your site. The sites structured by the group of engineers at Tvisha are easy to use with appealing plans and educational substance, to catch the eye of clients. The UI and UX of sites planned by them drive organizations towards remaining on top in the midst of the furious challenge in the business. They recognize the accurate prerequisite of the customer and creates sites according to customers' necessities that take your organizations all around.

Konstant Infosolutions: Konstant Infosolutions-a prestigious website composition improvement organization, is in the calling of giving a wide scope of web and portable arrangements on top of customer necessities worldwide since 2003. Their group of exceptionally talented IT experts experienced in conveying trend-setting innovation arrangements over a few businesses. They offer the top tier site advancement administrations, which are magnificently customized for your organizations inside your spending limit and time span.

WillowTree: WillowTree-a main web and application improvement organization built up in the year 2008, is serving the customers with their responsive site administrations for the top brands in the market like Johnson&Johnson, TimeWarner, Pepsico, and AOL. The applications and site planned by their group of expert advancement factor adaptability, superior, cost-viability, client-driven structure, vigorous improvement to fathom your most unpredictable business challenges. Huge Drop Inc: Big Drop Inc is a top website architecture and advancement firm situated in the home office of New York City established in the year 2012.

They offer adequate web improvement administrations to upgrade the ROI for your business by building an innovative site. Their group of architects and engineers makes front line sites that success grants and furthermore manage the customers through their inventive work process released while building up a site.

Fingent Technologies: Fingent Technologies- an overwhelming web improvement organization, who empower your business accomplishment through their venture web and application advancement administrations appropriate for your business needs. They convey modern online arrangements inside the financial limit and time for all customers crosswise over business spaces. They are capable of conveying custom web applications to business pioneers all around.

Shrouded Brains: Being a well-perceived website architecture and improvement organization in Hyderabad, Hidden Brains offers compelling web architecture and advancement administrations for a developing scope of organizations crosswise over assorted verticals. They serve their customers with testing and coordinating innovations. Their group of master engineers demonstrated a reputation by giving custom administrations, high-caliber and effective expectations dependent on the customer prerequisite.

Contus: Contus-a remarkable web improvement organization built up in the year 2008, is serving the customers with perfect web answers for different organizations and various businesses. Their group of expert designers fabricates the sites that improve your image, draw in worldwide clients, and give you higher business transformation with uncommon responsive subjects to pull in the customers.

Tutor Mate: Mentor Mate is a notable website architecture organization rendering innovative web advancement administrations for both the new companies and built up brands comprehensively. With over 16 years of involvement with the field of creating, they offer their administrations for different advanced stages and gadgets like Android, IOS, Windows and work area. NMG

Technologies: As a main web improvement organization in India, NMG advancements offer great web answers for your business. They fabricate a staggeringly incredible and adaptable site according to the business procedure of the customers. Their exceptionally experienced group of advanced specialists are committed to building superb items and sites for an industry. Iflexion: Iflexion-a momentous and built up web improvement organization from Texas, offers propelled website composition administrations and endeavor web applications for various entrances. Their uniquely arranged administrations of programming creation and execution help them to keep up a long haul client association with top MNCs like eBay, Cisco, Philips, Adidas, and Xerox. Their group of web engineers makes the top tier site convincing your business administrations.

5 Unknown Facts about Website Development for Business Owners

Is it accurate to say that you are a new business and attempting to begin an online business? You're above all else prerequisite is a decent Website Development Company. So as to begin an online business, first, you have to look out for the correct Web Development Company. Web improvement is the way toward coding and scrambling a standard scripting language to fabricate a site through programming. There is nothing to stress over as long your site is performing great and bringing you more guests. A business should begin stressing just if the site neglects to meet the objectives.

Just a couple of organizations see well what really occurs in the background of creating and refreshing a site. Nonetheless, as a site proprietor, a business ought to consistently attempt to comprehend the realities about site improvement.

1. The site ought to be refreshed after like clockwork:

With the consistent advancement in the field of site structuring and computerized promoting, you have to change the plan of your site to keep it appealing for various clients. A web improvement organization must think about the most recent coding gauges, program capacity updates and web search tool calculations. On the off chance that your site isn't refreshed, you may neglect to show your business effectively in an internet browser making antagonistic outcomes for your online business.

An obsolete site is consistently at danger of not showing the right outcomes in the program of the clients, bringing about sudden organizing issues and not bringing compelling web crawler results. A site gets the antiquated following two years and the site engineers need to patch up its plan. A redid web architecture may have the option to bring wanted business results to a client.

2. Web architecture tells the clients where they should center:

Sites that are effective have a format that can be effectively filtered by the internet browsers. On the off chance that your guests are not ready to find the key data on your site immediately then they are probably going to leave. In this manner, organizations should Hire Website Development Company to make destinations that are anything, but difficult to stack and explore giving guest's most significant data.

3. Your site appears to be unique on others' gadgets:

At the point when you see your site utilizing your PC on Google Chrome, it appears to be unique when you see it utilizing a companion's PC through the Safari internet browser. What your site resembles in a program depends totally on parsing and rendering, or in transit programs interpret code and show it on the screen of your gadget.

There are times when a program will stack a code in a particular request, while, now and then programs won't perceive a specific code by any stretch of the imagination. Because of the distinctions in programs, it gets dubious for the site improvement organizations to make a site to give an extraordinary encounter to the guests.

For the most part, the site designers are familiar with the programming dialects like HTML, CSS, PHP, and others. One of the most well known coding dialects utilized by the engineers is PHP, for the most part, utilized for explaining program issues and potential obstacles. A PHP Web Development Company ensures your site looks incredible and works appropriately on all the internet browsers. It's their principal occupation to recognize the potential issues and build up fixes for the issues before a site is propelled.

4. Pictures can put a positive just as negative effect on your web architecture:

Pictures can either represent the moment of truth the exhibition of a site. These are an amazing piece of a business site and whenever utilized inappropriately they can harm a site's presentation. In the event that you will put an enormous picture on your site, it will drastically hinder the heap time of your site. On the off chance that a guest needs to stand by long to stack a page, there is a likelihood that they will get anxious and leave your site.

In the event that as a business you have to guarantee that a sight and sound substance on your site connect with the guest and doesn't make them anxious, you ought to ask your Web Development Services to utilize pictures that are upgraded for the site. A picture advanced for a site will guarantee your page stacks rapidly and offers the guests with rich picture content.

5. Your site's code impacts your web crawler positioning:

You may have the most alluring web architecture in the whole world, yet it won't make any difference in the event that it has no guests. One of the approaches to guarantee your group of spectators discovers your site all the more effective is having a decent code. At the point when individuals look out for catchphrases in an internet searcher they need to get accurate outcomes, and for this web improvement organizations need to ensure they are utilizing a decent source code for a site. The source code utilized influences the web index positioning of your site.

Your site should be the most alluring site on the web on the off chance that you need more guests to contact you. Your business will never be affected by an appealing site, however, just the quantity of guests will do it for you.

Why Website Design and Development is Important and How it Helps in Making your Business Profitable?

With the appearance of new innovation, it is very barely noticeable out on regarded openings accessible. This circumstance is far more detestable when one doesn't have the aptitude to tap on these changes. All things considered, this is the situation for organizations, which have restricted information on site improvement and structure.

Let's be honest, site administrations have colossally changed how the business functions. Along these lines, for genuine business people or organizations wishing to know the significance of sites this article gives only that.

The following are the significant advantages of site advancement and website architecture.

Makes route simple

With regard to having an effective online stage, the client must appreciate the simple route. Basically, data gave on the site ought to be anything, but difficult to get to. Therefore, it is normal that the pages have quick stacking rates.

In this manner, the site is required to offer alternatives to additionally help in route. This envelops the incorporation of a hunt box. Here, the clients get the opportunity to type on the pursuit device and rapidly be coordinated to the segment. It is through commendable website composition that a designer's site accomplishes this.

Besides building up the site, the engineer is encouraged to normally test the pages for simplicity of route. This is to dispose of or resolve bugs that may hamper the simplicity of stacking site pages. Keep in mind, on the off chance that a site has great route abilities, at that point, it is ensured of progressively natural traffic.

Get the opportunity to win with SEO

Site improvement has become a basic viewpoint to see with regards to the site. With a great many sites challenging to the top in web crawler results pages (SERPs), web crawlers needed to acquaint a route with list destinations.

All things considered, it is through web advancement and plans that one gets the opportunity to accomplish a higher positioning. Here, parameters, for example, title labels, utilization of catchphrases, picture enhancement, connecting among others are considered. This infers the site fulfills every one of the guidelines required by be positioned top.

Hence, it is through streamlining that the site becomes easy to understand. Besides having the site, the website admins get the opportunity to hold genuinely necessary clients. Under this, the web designer is required to incorporate highlights, for example, "Embolden".

This further involves the need to have oversimplified plans on the pages. In this manner, you get the opportunity to learn at the normal stacking speeds. It is through this improvement that the site shows up when various inquiries are made. So the site gets more taps on list items.

Give visual substance on the site

Truth is stated, selling theoretical items and administrations can be awkward. This is additionally confused when an organization just gives huge amounts of content about their forte. It is here that site advancement flavors things up.

By reaching an expert website specialist, the entrepreneur gets the chance to pick the pictures to utilize. Moreover, the undertaking has the opportunity to pick the number of promotion recordings and pictures. This will be guided by the advancement of web indexes.

The value of utilizing visual substance is that it furnishes the clients with an unmistakable image of what the item resembles. Clearly, not all clients comprehend the administrations or items offered through content. So the consideration of pictures makes it easy to drive the message home.

Other than this, the utilization of pictures on the site effectively catches the consideration of the perusers. Prior to perusing the content, clients are regularly enthused about the picture. This improves the odds of having more clients to the site.

By the by, website admins are encouraged to abstain from stuffing the visual information. This is on the grounds that it makes it hard for the client to translate. It likewise brings down the positioning of the site of site improvement. So it is essential to direct the utilization of symbolism.

Increment the deals

Business thriving is profoundly tied down on the number of offers made. All things considered, making a site can viably help a business dare to draw in more deals. As indicated by Statista, internet business exercises are foreseen to develop by 21.3% constantly in 2019. This demonstrates deals on sites are pulling in more clients.

These days, more entrepreneurs are racing to direct their exchanges on the web. This is on the grounds that they have detected the extraordinary chance to profit by online deals. The expansion in deals goes connected at the hip with the developing number of clients.

To additionally advance the business, website admins are urged to incorporate updates. It is through updates and redesigns that the site capacities are smoothened. In addition, it shows the customers that the brand is committed to offering commendable administrations and data.

Another approach to improve the business is by including advancements. Here, you get the chance to make the truly necessary fluff among clients. This reproduces into more deals. Furthermore, this gives clients the feeling that they can procure reasonable items from the organization. In this way, all exercises on the site increase the value of the business somehow.

Pull in lifetime customers to your business

As the organization tries to spread its wings and grow, it is the principal to have faithful clients. In any case, this can be an overwhelming errand particularly when the business visionary uses poor strategies to accomplish this. It is now that the advancement and planning of the site help out.

The measurements recovered from the webpage empower website admins to screen the action of clients. Here, it is conceivable to feature the clients that have persistently upheld the brand. In the wake of pinpointing them, the entrepreneur should utilize inventive approaches to hold these clients.

One creative alternative is compensating them with blessing vouchers and prizes. This will give them more motivation to get to your administrations or items. Keep in mind, it is through the site that the entrepreneur guarantees no reliable client is forgotten about.

Another interesting thing about lifetime clients is that they can showcase the brand. So they get to in a roundabout way work for the organization. This additionally lessens the expense of showcasing.

Contact more customers

One of the fundamental objectives of setting up a venture is to develop regarding client base. All things considered, there is a horde of approaches to accomplish this, however, everyone has various outcomes. With regard to web advancement and plan, there are some significant achievements accomplished.

The first is that it puts the brand name out there. Basically, when the site is accessible on Worldwide Web then the organization is on a worldwide stage. This implies the little-realized undertaking can be looked at and give items to faraway clients.

It is these administrations that guide to decrease the separation for the clients to get to the exercises. Here, there are different alternatives, for example, acquiring or requesting the item on the site. Besides, the organization still stays in contact with neighborhood clients. Incredible right!

Improving client commitment

Expectedly, a venture was facilitated in a physical structure. Be that as it may, circumstances are different as more administrations have gotten computerized. It is thus that business visionaries are urged to create heavenly sites.

In this stage, it is very simple to keep up a decent affinity with the end client. This involves recovering criticism on the administrations and items advertised. So you can collaborate with them and give imperative reactions to the inquiries inquired. Also, there is no restriction on the hour of action. Via mechanizing the administrations on the site, customers are ensured of nonstop administrations.

Additionally, under client commitment, the blog or website proprietor can update clients as often as possible consistently. For example, on the off chance that new value charges are presented, at that point clients are among the first to know.

Ingenious in showcasing and publicizing

For new companies, having items and administrations out there is principal in making progress. All things considered, showcasing systems prove to be useful in selling the brand. Contrasted with strategies, for example, the utilization of principle media and bulletins, site improvement is pocket-accommodating.

It is through this online stage that an organization can show all pertinent data. This incorporates; items/administrations offered, area, evaluating, notoriety, contacts among others. The website admin can advantageously post appealing ideas on the site.

Curiously, it is simpler to refresh astounding limits and offers on the site. So there is no vacation in trusting that the promotion will be set up. A similar case applies when the organization wishes to pull down a blog entry or advert.

Also, the business adventure can work with a given figure. I don't get this' meaning? Basically, through SEO the business can realize where to put more accentuation. Moreover, the site gives cutting-edge data on the most recent commercial in the market.

Streamlining the brand

While presenting a site for the organization, it is essential that the brand name be reliable. It is through site advancement and website composition this is practiced. Here, the website admin will make a particular brand name that will be included on all the web crawlers. So there is no variety paying little respect to whether the site is on Bing or Google.

Besides, the brand logo and name are comparable all through. This diminishes the odds of disarray with other aggressive brands. This additionally streams down to the issue of consistency. It is foreseen that the organization keeps up a consistent following of their clients.

In the event of rebranding, the website admin ought to guarantee that the due strategy is pursued. When this is considered, at that point, the web crawlers will consequently refresh the records. In this way, when clients look for the brand to get the chance to get to the correct thing.

CHAPTER 9

AWS Storage Services

Distributed storage is a basic part of distributed computing, holding the data utilized by applications. Enormous information examination, information distribution centers, Internet of Things, databases, and reinforcement and document applications all depend on some type of information stockpiling design. Distributed storage is commonly increasingly dependable, adaptable, and secure than conventional on-premises stockpiling frameworks.

AWS offers a total scope of distributed storage administrations to help both application and authentic consistence prerequisites. Select from article, document, and square stockpiling administrations just as cloud information relocation alternatives to begin planning the establishment of your cloud IT condition.

IDC_Corporate_Logo

AWS Storage Portfolio Overview

Adapt more in an IDC whitepaper that assesses the AWS stockpiling portfolio, what's more, it investigates the Total Cost of Ownership for AWS distributed storage.

Get the IDC Whitepaper

AWS Cloud Storage Products

In the event that you need:

Think about Using:

Constant neighborhood stockpiling for Amazon EC2, for social and NoSQL databases, information warehousing, venture applications, Big Data preparing, or reinforcement and recovery Amazon Elastic Block Store

(Amazon EBS)

A straightforward, versatile, flexible record framework for Linux-based outstanding tasks at hand for use with AWS Cloud administrations and on-premises assets. It is worked to scale on request to petabytes without disturbing applications, developing and contracting consequently as you include and evacuate records, so your applications have the capacity they need – when they need it. Amazon Elastic File System

(Amazon EFS)

A completely overseen document framework that is upgraded for figure serious remaining tasks at hand, for example, superior registering, AI, and media information handling work processes, and is consistently

incorporated with Amazon S3   Amazon
FSx for Luster

A completely overseen local Microsoft Windows document framework based on Windows Server so you can without much of a stretch move your Windows-based applications that require record stockpiling to AWS, including full help for the SMB convention and Windows NTFS, Active Directory (AD) coordination, and Distributed File System (DFS). Amazon FSx for Windows File Server

An adaptable, sturdy stage to make information available from any Internet area, for a client, created content, dynamic document, serverless figuring, Big Data stockpiling or reinforcement and recovery Amazon Simple Storage Service

(Amazon S3)

Profoundly reasonable long haul stockpiling classes that can trade tape for document and administrative compliance Amazon Glacier and Amazon S3 Glacier Deep Archive

A half and half stockpiling cloud expanding your on-premises condition with Amazon distributed storage, for blasting, tiering or migration AWS Storage Gateway

An arrangement of administrations to help streamline and quicken moving information of various types and sizes into and out of the AWS cloud

Cloud Data Migration Services

A completely overseen reinforcement administration that makes it simple to incorporate and mechanize the back up of information crosswise over AWS benefits in the cloud just as on-premises utilizing the AWS Storage Gateway.

5 Awesome AWS Storage Types

Amazon Web Services (AWS) has become the most famous cloud administration supplier as of late, as organizations understand the estimation of re-appropriating their answers for a confided in the supplier. Amazon has earned its notoriety by furnishing a top-quality help with its tech contributions. The organization furnishes moderate stockpiling with versatility and dependability that is unequaled among cloud contenders.

Another viewpoint that puts AWS in front of the challenge is its numerous alternatives. With different stockpiling arrangements accessible, organizations can without much of a stretch pick the arrangement that meets their remarkable needs. Here are five of our most loved AWS stockpiling types.

Amazon S3

Versatility is the top objective of Amazon S3, making this arrangement perfect for organizations that have fluctuating stockpiling needs consistently. S3 likewise coordinates with a wide assortment of outsider applications, which is a major assistance to organizations that back and forth movement.

Organizations that pick S3 will likewise find that the arrangement's 99.99 percent accessibility implies their records are practically constantly accessible when they need them. The entirety of this at a moderate value that can support a little or medium-sized business remain inside its budgetary imperatives.

Amazon Glacier

Reasonableness is the large draw of Glacier, which is advertised as very minimal effort stockpiling. In any case, Glacier is intended for putting away information that shouldn't be recovered all the time. This arrangement is perfect for end clients who have a need to file enormous volumes of information that they'll infrequently get to, if at any time.

Amazon EFS

Amazon's Elastic File System (EFS) was the main item to work with a few Elastic Compute Cloud (EC2) cases. EFS offers executives the chance to allow explicit document consents over their stockpiling. Like different choices, EFS scales to fulfill a business' needs starting with one month then onto the next, yet it is somewhat more expensive than different alternatives.

This will be the best answer for organizations with a substantial interest in record stockpiling, just as associations that work with an assortment of documents and applications, including content administration, venture applications, and media.

Amazon EBS

Versatile Block Store (EBS) is intended to be utilized related to Amazon EC2, with information just storable when the two are associated. These points of confinement adaptability, making it a superior answer for organizations that have consistent stockpiling needs in light of the fact that extra space should be obtained.

The EBS pay-per-utilize model can help set aside a few organization's cash, however, since they'll pay for what they use. Because of its attention to consistency and low inertness, EBS is perfect for organizations that run requesting applications like information examination programming and SQL databases.

AWS Snowball

The present information overwhelming IT situations imply that data frequently should be moved starting with one spot then onto the next. Snowball is intended to make such moves simple without causing galactic system use charges. Rather than paying an extravagant engineer to compose code to push an exchange, administrators just move information utilizing the Snowball machine, without any points of confinement.

CHAPTER 10

Big Data Services

Large Data Services to Make a Big Difference

For a long time, we have been giving a full scope of large information administrations: counseling, execution, support and oversaw examination, to enable organizations to get important bits of knowledge out of their enormous information, break down interconnected issues and discover their main drivers, just as manufacture dependable forecasts.

Features About ScienceSoft

Large information accomplices

During 30 years in information examination and information science, we have been fulfilling organizations' assorted diagnostic needs (counting the requirement for cutting edge investigation), which makes us completely comprehend the change you're experiencing.

We hold organizations with Microsoft, Amazon, Oracle and other tech pioneers to keep pace with the mechanical progressions and the development of the information investigation scene.

We have 6 Microsoft Gold skills, including Data Analytics and Data Platform.

In 2018, we were named among top large information specialists by The Manifest.

Don't hesitate to demand extra data about our enormous information administrations custom-fitted to your venture.

Get in touch with the US

Huge Data Services We Offer

As any large information arrangement has the business and mechanical angles interweaved, we generally relegate an undertaking group comprising of both business investigators and innovation specialists to render huge information administrations.

Enormous information usage counseling

Is it true that you are intending to actualize a major information arrangement or totally redo the current one? We configuration cloud, on-premises, and a half and half arrangements that convert your large information into noteworthy experiences. That is the thing that we'll furnish you with:

A nitty-gritty guide for 3, 5 or 7 years that characterizes the means you should take to get key, strategic, and brisk successes through huge information controlled operational, client, business procedure and misrepresentation recognition investigation.

Proposals on the most proficient method to deal with the nature of the information.

A usage system and an arrangement.

A rundown of potential moves identified with large information usage and the approaches to illuminate them.

A client selection technique
An elevated level design with the recommended innovation stack

A proof of idea (for complex tasks)

Large information improvement counseling

On the off chance that you aren't totally happy with your current huge information arrangement, we make your individual improvement guide. Thusly, we dispose of the current issues (both the conspicuous ones that you advise us regarding and the shrouded ones that we inspire dependent on our experience). The new idea configuration is expected to amplify your examination potential. For instance, we can prescribe consolidating information science to empower progressed investigation or including reports that give additional bits of knowledge.

Enormous information execution

We convey enormous information arrangements that normally include the accompanying design parts: an information lake, an information distribution center, ETL forms, OLAP 3D squares, reports, and dashboards. We set up information quality administration and information security rehearses. We prepare and apply information science models, with its machine and profound learning calculations, to let organizations appreciate the high precision of expectations.

Huge information support

Enormous information support

We give the organization of your enormous information arrangement that incorporates such exercises as refreshing programming, including new clients, taking care of consents, just as information organization that incorporates, however, isn't restricted to information cleaning, reinforcement, and recuperation. We likewise can direct standard wellbeing checks to guarantee that your huge information arrangement is as yet secure, disappointment safe and profoundly performing. Additionally, we can screen your answer's presentation to recognize issues as ahead of schedule as could be expected under the circumstances (even before they happen) and investigate them.

Huge information oversaw investigation administrations

Searching for a solid specialist co-op to re-appropriate your large information investigation? We set up straightforward cooperation dependent on KPIs, assuming liability for the estimation of investigation experiences that you get. We make and bolster the foundation for your huge information arrangement, get your information removed and cleaned, and AI models (assuming any) prepared and tuned.

What's more, what stays for you is to profit by canny predefined and specially appointed reports that become accessible inside two or three weeks after our participation begins. Furthermore, we persistently improve the arrangement, altering it to the changing needs of your business.

CHAPTER 11

Notification Services

10 Best Push Notification Services and Tools [2019]

Fruitful message pop-ups normally get up to 2x higher navigate rates than messages do.

Truth is stranger than fiction – on the off chance that you use them effectively, you'll be getting twofold the measure of individuals to see your substance contrasted with on the off chance that you had sent your message to your group of spectators in an email.

They are an incredible method to support commitment with your group of spectators, and they're accessible both on the web and in versatile applications.

In any case, in case you're perusing this you most likely definitely know the advantages of Push Notifications.

Presently you simply need to pick the correct message pop-up administration for your business.

We've gathered the most well known pop-up message administrations into this manual to assist you with picking the correct one for you.

How about we get into the post

Picking a Push Notification Service For Your Website and App

Picking the correct pop-up message administration is going to make your commitment methodology a lot simpler, as it'll be anything, but difficult to set up and send warnings to your connection with clients.

A portion of these pop-up message administrations are more outstanding than others, yet all have solid usefulness. We've remembered data for their estimating alternatives, as some cook more to littler organizations, while others target high development or venture organizations.

In any case, it will merit investigating the choices before settling on the administration you'll pick.

Here are the push administrations we will be taking a gander at:

OneSignal

Google Firebase

LeanPlum

Pushbots

PushCrew

Carrier

CataPush

Message pop-ups for WordPress

PushAlert

Brilliant Notification WordPress Plugin

OneSignal

OneSignal is one of the main message pop-up administrations. It's utilized by organizations like Uber, Adobe, Conde Nast, Skyscanner, to give some examples, so on the off chance that you go with OneSignal, you'll be following some great people's example. It's additionally allowed to utilize.

Like Google or Facebook, the information your notices give to OneSignal is the explanation it's allowed to utilize, anyway they won't send advertisements to your clients.

You can send portable pop-up messages, web pop-up messages, in-application warnings, just as email notices.

Your MobiLoud versatile application can coordinate straightforwardly with OneSignal, which means it's the perfect arrangement in the event that you are wanting to utilize them both on your site, and in your portable application.

Value: Free (in addition to paid help alternatives on the off chance that you need more help)

Google Firebase

Just as having a large group of different highlights, Google Firebase lets you send Push Notifications to application clients.

Like some other Google business instruments, it's anything, but difficult to utilize and does as guaranteed, yet as it's not extraordinarily intended for Push Notifications (not at all like a portion of the other pop-up message administrations referenced here), you can anticipate a few trade-offs.

So, what you probably won't get in additional highlights and usefulness, Google compensates for with examination mix.

Value: Free

Leadplum

Leanplum covers the entire range of a group of spectators interchanges: email advertising, versatile notices, application inbox messages, and then some.

It's one of the main versatile advertising stages, offering a total toolbox including all that you'll requirement for scaling an effective message pop-up methodology.

Furthermore, it comes total with A/B testing, mechanization devices, and pop-up message personalization includes so you can get considerably increasingly out of your ongoing client notices.

Value: Contact them for a custom statement dependent on your necessities

PushBots

PushBots pop-up messages

PushBots is a pop-up message administration with a few extremely incredible qualities.

For one, it's stuffed with robotization. While there will come times when you have to physically push out warnings, there's a lot of it you might need to streamline and this application enables you to do that.

The investigation gave by PushBots is another specific quality, equaling what you'd find in Google Analytics.

Value: Starts at $29/mo.

PushCrew

PushCrew pop-up messages

For those of you who haven't fabricated a versatile application, PushCrew would be an incredible arrangement as it bargains exclusively in web and portable web message pop-ups.

All things considered, personalization is accessible, however, it concentrates more on the sorts of practices and kinds of triggers you'd use on a site.

Value: Free up to 2,000 endorsers, at that point premium plans are accessible

Aircraft

Urban Airship - 10 Best Push Notification Services and Tools [2019]

Aircraft (once in the past known as Urban Airship) practices exclusively in the portable correspondence experience, which implies it doesn't simply help with versatile application push.

It likewise handles things like SMS messages, email, and portable wallets. While the prescient investigation and AI advancement are alluring highlights to have, this sort of administration accompanies a cost.

Aircraft is gone for big business clients, and on the off chance that you go with them as your message pop-up supplier, you'll never feel like your shy of highlights to utilize.

Value: Basic arrangement begins at $99/mo.

Catapush

Catapush message pop-up administration

Catapush is a straightforward conveyance API enabling you to send message pop-ups identifying with your web application. It's intended to be perfect for sending information-driven, value-based notices dependent on client action on your site or application.

For each warning, you can see constant statuses and conveyance affirmation. As you would expect, you can likewise send rich media in your warnings.

CHAPTER 12

AWS Security

AWS Security Hub gives you a far-reaching perspective on your high-need security alarms and consistence status crosswise over AWS accounts. There is a scope of ground-breaking security apparatuses available to you, from firewalls and endpoint assurance to helplessness and consistence scanners. Be that as it may, generally this leaves your group exchanging to and fro between these instruments to manage hundreds, and some of the time thousands, of security alarms each day.

With Security Hub, you presently have a solitary spot that totals, arranges, and organizes your security cautions, or discoveries, from various AWS administrations, for example, Amazon GuardDuty, Amazon Inspector, and Amazon Macie, just as from AWS Partner arrangements. Your discoveries are outwardly abridged on coordinated dashboards with noteworthy charts and tables. You can likewise persistently screen your condition utilizing mechanized consistency checks dependent on the AWS best practices and industry norms your association pursues.

CHAPTER 13

AWS Database

Step by step instructions to make and associate with your AWS RDS (Relational Database Services) occasion

This blog will stroll through the making of an AWS RDS occurrence utilizing the AWS reassure. Reasons, why one would be keen on putting away and keeping up their database utilizing AWS, include:

Constrained extra room on your nearby machine

Capacity or programming confinements to what you can store on your work's server

Want for expanded security

Want for progressively effective information pipeline capacities

Mechanization of database upkeep, for example, programming updates, patches, and fiasco recuperation

In case you're new to working with huge information, a famous application for little to medium information stockpiling you may almost certainly be comfortable with is MS Access. MS Access can store 2GB of information, less the space required for framework objects.

On the paid levels, AWS RDS can store terabytes of information. In the AWS complementary plan, you have 20 GB of general stockpiling.

Coming up next is a rundown of MS Office Maximums:

MS Access is a mainstream database application in numerous enterprises. In the event that your present information venture is exceeding it, AWS RDS can give a minimal effort evidence of-idea to help a business case to receive AWS RDS, or a database programming like PostgreSQL, contingent upon what meets your requirements.

Whatever your purpose behind checking out RDS, the initial step is to make an example.

Explore to RDS utilizing the AWS support, click "Make Database". The main screen will ask you which Engine you'd prefer to utilize.

I picked PostgreSQL, yet you can pick whichever you're generally alright with.

2. Pick Dev/Test Environment (Free-level qualified)

3. Determine Instance. Defaults ought to be fine, for our motivations, we'll be hoping to remain complementary plan qualified

4. Defaults will be incredible, until you get to this one in "Design Advanced Settings", ensure you can oversee qualifications utilizing IAM clients and jobs

5. You'll likewise need to enter a secret phrase:

6. Amazing! You've made your database! Explore to a screen that resembles this by clicking "Cases" as an afterthought board

On the off chance that you look down or CTRL+"F" 'endpoint' it will take you to your occasion endpoint, which will get significant later.

7. Presently on the off chance that you neglected to make a secret phrase for your client: Go to your RDS Dashboard, select your

RDS case, Click Instance activities, and select "Alter"

I utilize this guide to give you that you have fresh opportunities.

8. In case you're making a change to your example later in the game, it will take you to a screen where you get the chance to pick between Applying it in a flash or during the following planned support window.

CHAPTER 14

AWS Security

Security and Compliance

Cloud security at AWS is the most elevated need. As an AWS client, you will profit by a server farm and system engineering worked to meet the prerequisites of the most security-delicate associations. Security in the cloud is a lot of like security in your on-premises server farms—just without the expenses of keeping up offices and equipment.

In the cloud, you don't need to oversee physical servers or capacity gadgets. Rather, you use programming based security instruments to screen and ensure the progression of data into and of out of your cloud assets.

A favorable position of the AWS Cloud is that it enables you to scale and enhance while keeping up a protected domain and paying just for the administrations you use. This implies you can have the security you need at a lower cost than in an on-premises condition.

As an AWS client, you acquire all the prescribed procedures of AWS strategies, engineering, and operational procedures worked to fulfill the prerequisites of our most security-delicate clients. Get the adaptability and nimbleness you need in security controls.

The AWS Cloud empowers a common obligation model. While AWS oversees the security of the cloud, you are liable for security in the cloud. This implies you hold control of the security you decide to execute to ensure your very own substance, stage, applications, frameworks, and systems no uniquely in contrast to you would in an on-location server farm.

AWS gives you direction and mastery through online assets, faculty, and accomplices. AWS furnishes you with warnings for current issues, in addition to you have the chance to work with AWS when you experience security issues.

You gain admittance to many instruments and highlights to assist you with meeting your security targets. AWS gives security-explicit instruments and highlights crosswise over system security, arrangement the executives, get to control, and information encryption.

At last, AWS situations are constantly inspected, with affirmations from accreditation bodies crosswise over geologies and verticals. In the AWS condition, you can exploit computerized apparatuses for resource stock and special access revealing.

Advantages of AWS Security

Guard Your Data: The AWS framework sets up solid shields to help ensure your protection. All information is put away in exceptionally secure AWS server farms.

Meet Compliance Requirements: AWS oversees many consistency programs in its framework. This implies sections of your consistence have just been finished.

Set aside Cash: Cut expenses by utilizing AWS server farms. Keep up the best quality of security without dealing with your own office

Scale Quickly: Security scales with your AWS Cloud use. Regardless of the size of your business, the AWS framework is intended to protect your information.

Consistence

AWS Cloud Compliance empowers you to comprehend the strong controls set up at AWS to keep up security and information insurance in the cloud. As frameworks are based on the AWS Cloud foundation, consistency obligations will be shared. By integrating administration centered, review neighborly assistance highlights with pertinent consistency or review norms, AWS Compliance empowering influences to expand on conventional projects. This causes clients to set up and work in an AWS security control condition.

The IT foundation that AWS gives to its clients is structured and oversaw in arrangement with best security rehearses and an assortment of IT security guidelines. Coming up next is a halfway rundown of confirmation programs with which AWS consents:

SOC 1/ISAE 3402, SOC 2, SOC 3

FISMA, DIACAP, and FedRAMP

PCI DSS Level 1

ISO 9001, ISO 27001, ISO 27017, ISO 27018

AWS gives clients a wide scope of data on its IT control condition in whitepapers, reports, confirmations, accreditations, and other outsider validations. More data is accessible in the Risk and Compliance whitepaper and the AWS Security Center.

CHAPTER 15

AWS Management Services

As big business clients move towards receiving the cloud at scale, some discover their kin need assistance and time to pick up AWS aptitudes and experience. AWS Managed Services (AMS) works AWS on your sake, giving a safe and agreeable AWS Landing Zone, a demonstrated venture working model, on-going cost improvement, and everyday foundation the executives.

By executing best practices to keep up your foundation, AWS Managed Services lessens your operational overhead and hazard. AWS Managed Services mechanizes normal exercises, for example, change demands, checking, fix the board, security, and reinforcement benefits, and gives full-lifecycle administrations to the arrangement, run, and bolster your framework. AWS Managed Services unburdens you from framework activities so you can coordinate assets toward separating your business.

CHAPTER 16

AWS Cost Management

Cloud innovation has changed how associations are organized. No place is this more obvious than in the cloud cost the executive's space. Here is a portion of the key changes that we've found in the manners that associations consider and represent their expenses:

Paying for assets that are utilized, regularly at granular units of utilization (for instance, running hours or bytes)

The capacity for anybody in an association to start assets whenever regularly as fast as a couple of moments

A consistently developing arrangement of cloud administrations and items from which to pick

AWS Cost Management devices give you perceivability into your AWS expenses and utilization. There is a scope of AWS Cost Management apparatuses to enable you to get to, compose, get, control, and enhance your expenses.

CHAPTER 17

AWS vs. Google Cloud Platform

At a High Level: AWS versus Google Cloud Platform

eWEEK RESOURCE PAGE: AWS and Google Cloud Platform, two of the three biggest distributed computing merchants, each have their very own qualities and shortcomings that make them proficient for various remaining burdens. Which may be best for your utilization case?

Online class:

On-Demand

Work area as-a-Service Designed for any Cloud? Nutanix Frame

Download the legitimate guide: Cloud Computing: Using the Cloud for Competitive Advantage

AWS.GCP

For most endeavors, choosing both an essential and optional cloud administration is currently a significant system. Late research shows that northward of 90 percent of endeavors and non-benefit associations are using at least two cloud administrations accounts. This is a major change over what was occurring just a couple of years prior when a few organizations were as yet hesitant to confide in their business information in any cloud application.

Cloud-specialist organizations, for example, Amazon Web Services, Microsoft Azure, Google, IBM, Dell EMC, Salesforce, Oracle and others are making it simpler all the ideal opportunity for clients to go back and forth or include or subtract limit or applications as required. These and different suppliers additionally keep concocting new and increasingly productive administrations for organizations to utilize, a significant number of which currently include man-made brainpower alternatives to make them progressively important.

Qualys is the cutting edge cloud application for unrivaled permeability and consistent security of open cloud foundation. Distinguish and resolve any vulnerabilities with an honor winning cloud stage over the cloud, on-premises, and cell phones. Attempt their first-class programming for nothing.

Why Discovery Is Critical to Multi-Cloud SuccessDownloadDownload Asset

Further perusing

Perceiving the Right Stuff in Cloud Security

HYCU Unveils New-Gen Backup, Recovery for Google Cloud...

In this article, we investigate two of the three biggest cloud administration suppliers on the planet: Amazon Web Services and Google Cloud Platform.

Go here to see a week's posting of the Top Cloud Computing Companies.

Go here to peruse eWEEK's Top Cloud Storage Companies list.

What we'll do here is analyze at a significant level and in a couple of various ways, these two worldwide distributed storage and processing administrations, in order to assist you with choosing the one that suits your organization as the most cost-and highlight effective one accessible.

AWS versus GCP: Key Similarities, Differences

To utilize an AWS administration, clients must pursue an AWS account. After they have finished this procedure, they can dispatch any help under their record inside Amazon's expressed points of confinement, and these administrations are charged to their particular record. If necessary, clients can make charging records and afterward make sub-accounts that move up to them. Along these lines, associations can imitate a standard authoritative charging structure.

Thus, GCP expects clients to set up a Google record to utilize its administrations. In any case, GCP arranges administration utilization by venture instead of by account. In this model, clients can make various, entirely separate activities under a similar record. In an authoritative setting, this model can be beneficial, enabling clients to make venture spaces for isolated divisions or gatherings inside an organization.

This model can likewise be valuable for testing purposes: when a client is finished with a task, the person can erase the venture, and the entirety of the assets made by that undertaking additionally will be erased.

AWS and GCP both have default delicate points of confinement on their administrations for new records. These delicate breaking points are not attached to specialized restrictions for a given assistance; rather, they are set up to assist keep false records from utilizing over the top assets, and to restrain hazard for new clients, preventing them from spending more than expected as they investigate the stage.

In the event that you find that your application has outgrown these points of confinement, AWS and GCP give direct approaches to connect with the fitting interior groups to raise the cutoff points on their administrations.

Asset Management Interfaces

AWS and GCP each give a direction line interface (CLI) for cooperating with the administrations and assets. AWS gives the Amazon CLI, and GCP gives the Cloud SDK. Each is a bound together CLI for all administrations, and each is cross-stage, with parallels accessible for Windows, Linux, and macOS. What's more, in GCP, you can utilize the Cloud SDK in your internet browser by utilizing Google Cloud Shell.

AWS and GCP additionally give online consoles. Each reassures enables clients to make, oversee, and screen their assets. The reassure for GCP is situated at https://console.cloud.google.com/.

Evaluating Processes Are Different

One territory where there is certainly not an outstanding contrast between these two market pioneers is in evaluating. AWS utilizes a pay-more only as costs arise model and charges clients every hour—and they pay for an entire hour, regardless of whether they utilize just a single moment of it. Google Cloud pursues a to-the-minute evaluating process.

Numerous specialists suggest that endeavors assess their open cloud needs individually and coordinate explicit applications and remaining tasks at hand with the merchant that offers the best fit for their needs. Every one of the main sellers has specific qualities and shortcomings that settle on them a decent decision for explicit ventures.

Along these lines, how about we get into more particulars.

What is AWS?

Amazon Web Services (AWS) is a cloud administration stage from Amazon, which gives benefits in various areas, for example, process, stockpiling, conveyance and other usefulness, which help the business to scale and develop. AWS uses these spaces as administrations, which can be utilized to make and convey various kinds of users in the cloud stage. These administrations are planned so that they work with one another and produce an adaptable and effective result.

AWS administrations are arranged into three sorts: foundation as a help (IaaS), programming as an assistance (SaaS) and stage as an assistance (PaaS). AWS was propelled in 2006 and become the most-obtained cloud stage among as of now accessible cloud stages. Cloud stages offer different favorable circumstances, for example, the board overhead decrease, cost minimization, and numerous others.

AWS Pros and Cons Based on User Feedback

Experts: Amazon's single greatest quality truly ended up being the way that it was first to advertise in 2006 and didn't have any genuine challenge for over two years. It supports this initiative by proceeding to put vigorously in its server farms and arrangements. This is the reason its rules the general population cloud advertise.

Gartner Research detailed in its Magic Quadrant for Cloud Infrastructure as a Service, Worldwide, that "AWS has been the piece of the overall industry pioneer in cloud IaaS for more than 10 years." Specifically, AWS has been the world head for more like 13 years, or as far back as it initially propelled its S3 (Simple Storage Service) in fall 2006.

Some portion of the purpose behind its ubiquity is positively the huge extent of its worldwide activities. AWS has an immense and developing cluster of accessible administrations, just as the most far-reaching system of overall server farms. Gartner has portrayed AWS as "The most develop, endeavor prepared (cloud administrations) supplier, with the most profound abilities for administering countless clients and assets."

CONS: Cost and information get to are Amazon's Achilles heels. While AWS routinely brings down its costs—truth be told, it has brought down them in excess of multiple times over the most recent quite a long while, which presumably implies they were too high to even think about beginning with. Numerous undertakings think that its hard to comprehend the organization's cost structure. They additionally make some hard memories dealing with these expenses viably when running a high volume of remaining tasks at hand on the administration. Also, clients, be careful: Be certain you comprehend the expenses of separating information and documents once they are in AWS's stockpiling control.

AWS will clarify everything in advance for you, however, realize that it's significantly simpler to begin a procedure and transfer records into the AWS cloud and access applications and administrations than to discover information and documents you need and move them to another server or capacity exhibit.

All in all, be that as it may, these cons are exceeded by Amazon's qualities since associations of all sizes keep on utilizing AWS for a wide assortment of remaining burdens.

Peruse client surveys of Amazon Web Services

For sure, the way that cloud frameworks share quite a bit of their innovation is a basic factor in their potential helplessness. At the point when one part is exploited, it opens the rest to misuse except if the best possible strides to restrict the hazard are taken ahead of time. Qualys offers the most extreme assurance with powerlessness the executives, web application checking, consistent observing, and the sky is the limit from there. Get your free preliminary.

What is Google Cloud Platform?

For as far back as 15 years, Google has been building one of the quickest, generally ground-breaking, and most excellent cloud foundations on earth. Inside, Google itself utilizes this framework for a few high-traffic and worldwide scale administrations, including Gmail, Maps, YouTube and Search. In light of the size and size of these administrations, Google has placed a great deal of work into advancing its framework and making a suite of apparatuses and administrations to oversee it adequately. GCP puts this framework and these administration assets readily available.

Characterizing GCP

Google Cloud was created by Google and propelled in 2008. It was written in Java, C++, Python including Ruby. It additionally gives the various administrations that are IaaS, PaaS and Serverless stage. Google cloud is sorted into various stages, for example, Google App Engine, Google Compute Engine, Google Cloud Datastore, Google Cloud Storage, Google Big Query (for investigation) and Google Cloud SQL. Google cloud stage offers significant level processing, stockpiling, systems administration and databases.

It additionally offers various choices for systems administration, for example, virtual private cloud, cloud CDN, cloud DNS, load adjusting and other discretionary highlights. It additionally offers the executives of huge information and the Internet of things (IoT) outstanding tasks at hand. Cloud

CHAPTER 18

AWS Certification

Associations need people with cloud abilities to help change their business. AWS Training and Certification encourages you to construct and approve your cloud abilities so you can get progressively out of the cloud. Our substance is worked by specialists at AWS and refreshed consistently to keep pace with AWS refreshes, so you can be certain you're learning the most recent and keeping your cloud aptitudes new.

We offer both computerized and study hall preparing, so you can decide to learn online at your own pace or take in best practices from an educator. Regardless of whether you are simply beginning, expanding on existing IT abilities, or honing your cloud information,

AWS Training and Certification can assist you with being increasingly successful and accomplish more in the cloud.

CHAPTER 19

AWS Tips And Tricks

20 Tips and Tricks to Make AWS Work to Your Advantage

Amazon Web Services, touted as a pioneer in the Cloud specialist organizations, has been a predictable leader in the IAAS and PAAS space. Associations independent of their size have picked AWS as their go-to Cloud specialist organization making it an undisputed contender in the zone of Cloud administrations. With the edge in the race to the top always augmenting among AWS and its nearest showcase rival, their power can be ascribed to their deliberately made market methodology.

AWS holds the top position in light of its ceaseless development approach methodology just as a disposition of growing accomplice biological system.

Let us dive further into every one of these traits that make AWS stick out so unequivocally in such a focused circumstance.

Persistent Innovation Strategy

In a limited capacity to focus time on the primary portion of this current year, AWS has effectively added 422 administrations to its effectively renowned portfolio. It has taken it further by incorporating examination and AI abilities into its contributions. This gives AWS a favorable position to remain side by side with the most recent cloud patterns and in front of its opposition.

Accomplice Ecosystem

AWS is additionally continually growing its accomplice biological system by adding a few tenable names to the rundown, which adds to its unwavering quality as a worldwide Cloud specialist organization. Aside from that, AWS is spreading its impressions over the world with a solid and reliable system.

As indicated by a CloudTech report, AWS proceeds with its position a worldwide pioneer in Cloud with over 45% overall piece of the overall industry when contrasted with its rivals like Microsoft, IBM, and Google.

The RightScale 2017 State of the Cloud Report repeats that AWS keeps on driving in broad daylight cloud reception.

In spite of the fact that AWS has thought of a heap of administrations, one can't resist the urge to see that the majority of its administrations are either under-used or undiscovered to their actual potential. The purpose of this under-usage is regularly the absence of ability and fundamental obliviousness. This article, along these lines, takes into account bits of knowledge from various client cases identified with AWS. The essential target is to offer your association a few hacks to spare expense on the cloud framework and oversee it viably.

We should investigate every one of these tips and deceives.

20 Tips and Tricks to Get the Most Out of AWS

1. Versatile IP can be a Free of Cost Feature

AWS furnishes one free Elastic IP with each running occasion. Notwithstanding, extra EIPs for that specific running occasion are regularly chargeable and it can cost you in specific situations. AWS charges its clients for EIPs in occurrences when they are either not related to any occasion or on the off chance that they are appended to a halted example. They guarantee that the halted cases don't have EIPs appended to them until required.

Then again, EIPs can be remapped for up to 100 times each month without acquiring any additional charge.

2. Spare Big by Judicious Use of ALBs

Standard and uncontrolled exemplary burden balancers can be inconvenient for an association's financial limit. According to insights, an association is paying, at any rate, $18 for each heap balancer. ALB acts as the hero in such circumstances. They are less expensive than exemplary burden balancers, however, ALB likewise bolsters way based directing, have based steering, and HTTP/2. AWS ECS successfully underpins ALB and can supplant up to 75 ELBs with single ALB by appropriate use. Be that as it may, ALBs just help HTTP and HTTPS. In this way, if organizations are utilizing TCP convention, they will, in any case, need to utilize ELB.

3. Record Aliases over the CNAME when Using Route 53

While utilizing CNAMEs for different administrations like ALB Cloudfront and so on., including an Alias record type over the CNAME gives some extra advantages. AWS doesn't charge for Alias records sets inquiries and Alias records the spare time as AWS Route53 naturally perceives changes in the record sets. Likewise, Alias's records sets are not obvious in answer from Route53 DNS servers making them progressively secure.

4. Pursue the Best Practices of EBS Provisioning

EBS volumes are a fundamental piece of the EC2 framework and need extraordinary consideration while provisioning. It is a superior practice to Start with littler estimated EBS volumes as AWS has as of late propelled highlight of resizing EBS volumes as and when the application requests. This takes care of the issue of provisioning bigger estimated EBS volumes at an underlying level remembering the future necessities. It never again expects one to plan personal times to overhaul their EBS volume limit. Notwithstanding, the order to secure a new EBS limit should be given physically. Since provisioned EBS volumes, for the most part, have a greater expense when contrasted with universally useful EBS volumes utilizing littler EBS volumes additionally saves money on cost.

5. Use Multi-AZ RDS for Effective Application Backup and Recovery

In the event of disappointment, AWS switches the equivalent RDS endpoint to the point of the backup machine, which can take as long as 30 seconds, however, the applications continue working consistently. Reinforcements and support are first performed to the backup occurrence, trailed by a programmed failover making the entire procedure smoother. Additionally, the IO movement isn't suspended while accepting reinforcements as they are taken from reserve case.

6. Arrange Multiple Alarms on Cloudwatch to Spike Notifications

Cloudwatch cautions are activated just when they rupture a certain limit. On the off chance that a measurement has just broken its edge esteem and informed a group, at that point the caution will advise for the subsequent time if a similar limit, doesn't have the choice for heightening an alert to an alternate group if that alert isn't settled in a stipulated time span. In this manner, to tap the AWS Cloudwatch to its fullest, design various cautions on Cloudwatch for a solitary occurrence at various time interims to advise various groups.

7. Make a point to Delete Snapshots while Deregistering AMIs

EBS depictions are put away in S3 and do acquire capacity costs. This implies the more AMIs made, the more you pay for the capacity cost. An AMI gets expelled from your record when you deregister the AMI yet their EBS doesn't get erased consequently. These are called zombies or vagrant previews as their parent AMI doesn't exist and gobble up the capacity costs. One needs to physically erase these depictions to free up some stockpiling to battle this issue.

8. Influence Compression at the Edge Feature in Cloudfront

Associations can utilize pressure at edge highlight of Cloudfront while serving web content. Cloudfront naturally packs the advantages and conveys the compacted substance to the customer sparing the information move cost as well as pace up the substance download. With this, you can legitimately pack and serve content from S3.

9. Productive utilization of S3 empowers higher investment funds

S3 can deliver enormous investment funds when managing huge estimated information by utilizing the S3 RRS (Reduced Redundancy Storage) and rare access administration. AWS keeps their information in a solitary district-sponsored up in numerous AZs and not in every one of the areas. This doesn't imply that the information is less secure. They can even now utilize RRS for some less basic information.

They can likewise utilize Glacier for the recording of information as Glacier underpins information recovery in no time flat.

10. Recreating Critical S3 Data

To recreate or reinforcement the basic S3 information to different districts, organizations currently have an element of cross-area replication of an S3 container to an alternate locale. When the information is transferred in the source container, it will naturally imitate the goal pail in an alternate district. This element just works with pails in an alternate locale and not in a similar area.

11. Spare Time and Effort while Data Retrieval from Glacier

The ice sheet is an exceptionally supportive element in the information recorded. In any case, information recovery from Glacier can be a costly issue. Despite the fact that the procedure is somewhat dull at the outset, however, the information that can be put as huge compressed documents ought to be put away in little pieces.

It is perfect to move information in little lumps rather than huge pieces on the grounds that it is simpler to reestablish a little measured document in little estimated lump than in a huge measured lump. This will likewise make it simpler to get to and at a littler expense as recovering an enormous information lump for a little record will have you pay the expense for the recovery of the whole huge information piece.

12. Abstain from utilizing T2 Instances in Production Environment

T2 examples shouldn't be utilized underway conditions as they are not intended to deal with constant generation outstanding burdens for the long term. Notwithstanding, the cases get a particular number of CPU credits every hour, which can be used at the hour of an overwhelming outstanding burden for quite a while. When the framework devours all its

CPU credits, at that point it will again go to its gauge execution, debasing any CPU serious strategic assignment running on the creation server.

Conclusion

AWS gives various productive, secure availability alternatives to assist you with benefiting from AWS when incorporating your remote systems with Amazon VPC. The alternatives gave in this whitepaper feature a few of the available choices and examples that clients have used to effectively coordinate their remote systems or numerous Amazon VPC systems. You can utilize the data gave here to decide the most fitting component for associating the foundation required to maintain your business paying little mind to where it is physically found or facilitated.

www.ingramcontent.com/pod-product-compliance
Lightning Source LLC
Chambersburg PA
CBHW071109050326
40690CB00008B/1167